Popular Mechanics

WHY A CURVEBALL CURVES

THE INCREDIBLE SCIENCE OF SPORTS

Popular Mechanics

WHY A CURVEBALL CURVES
THE INCREDIBLE SCIENCE OF SPORTS

edited by FRANK VIZARD

foreword by ROBERT LIPSYTE

HEARST BOOKS
A division of Sterling Publishing Co., Inc.

New York / London
www.sterlingpublishing.com

Copyright © 2008 by Hearst Communications, Inc.

Book design by Agustin Chung

Library of Congress Cataloging-in-Publication Data
Popular mechanics why a curveball curves : the incredible science of sports / edited by Frank Vizard.
      p. cm.
  Includes index.
  ISBN-13: 978-1-58816-475-9
  ISBN-10: 1-58816-475-6
  1. Sports sciences. I. Vizard, Frank. II. Popular mechanics (Chicago, Ill. : 1959)
III. Title: Why a curveball curves.
  GV558.P67 2008
  613.7'1--dc22

10 9 8 7 6 5 4 3 2 1

Published by Hearst Books
A Division of Sterling Publishing Co., Inc.
387 Park Avenue South, New York, NY 10016

Popular Mechanics and Hearst Books are trademarks of Hearst Communications, Inc.

www.popularmechanics.com

For information about custom editions, special sales, premium and corporate purchases, please contact Sterling Special Sales Department at 800-805-5489 or specialsales@sterlingpub.com.

Distributed in Canada by Sterling Publishing
c/o Canadian Manda Group, 165 Dufferin Street
Toronto, Ontario, Canada M6K 3H6

Distributed in Australia by Capricorn Link (Australia) Pty. Ltd.
P.O. Box 704, Windsor, NSW 2756 Australia

Manufactured in China

Sterling ISBN 13: 978-1-58816-475-9
        ISBN 10: 1-5886-475-6

Contents

THE CONTRIBUTORS

THE SPECIALISTS

Matt Bahr: Kicker for six National Football League (NFL) teams between 1979 and 1995. He kicked the winning field goal in Super Bowl XXV as the New York Giants defeated the Buffalo Bills—the final score was 20–19.

Bob Bowman: Head coach for the University of Michigan swim team and the 2001 and 2003 swimming coach of the year. Bowman coached Olympic swimming great Michael Phelps to a record-setting eight swimming medals in the 2004 Olympics.

Buzz "The Shot Doctor" Braman: Shooting coach in the National Basketball Association (NBA) for more than ten years, working with such teams as the Philadelphia 76ers and the Orlando Magic. In the off-season, he runs shooting camps for players of all ages.

Peter Brancazio: Professor Emeritus of Physics, Brooklyn College, The City University of New York, and author of *Sport Science*.

Dean Golich and Craig Griffin: Coaches, Carmichael Training Systems, Colorado Springs, Colorado.

Jeff Huber: Head diving coach at Indiana University and an Olympic diving coach in 2000 and 2004.

Jim Kaat: Major-league pitcher for 25 years, left-hander Kaat won 283 games and earned sixteen Gold Gloves while playing for the Washington Senators, Minnesota Twins, Chicago White Sox, Philadelphia Phillies, New York Yankees, and St. Louis Cardinals. He retired in 2006 after a second career as a baseball broadcaster for the YES Network and WCBS.

Lou Piniella: Manager of the Chicago Cubs and a former player for the Kansas City Royals, New York Yankees, Baltimore Orioles, and Cleveland Indians. He has also managed the New York Yankees, Seattle Mariners, Cincinnati Reds, and Tampa Bay Devil Rays.

Laura Stamm: Taught hockey players with the Los Angeles Kings, New York Rangers, New York Islanders, New Jersey Devils, and the U.S. Olympic team how to increase their skating speed. She is the author of *Power Skating* and operates skating clinics across the United States.

Dr. Joe Vigil: Legendary coach for distance running in track-and-field events and cross-country. His association with the U.S. Olympic team dates back to 1968. At the 2004 Olympic Games in Athens, Greece, he coached marathoner Deena Kastor to a Bronze Medal. He was named National Coach of the Year fourteen times and produced 425 All-Americans.

ADDITIONAL CONTRIBUTORS

A. A. Albelli
John Bakke
Stephen A. Booth
Davin Coburn
Tom Colligan
Aubrey O. Cookman Jr.
John G. Falcioni
Steve Flink
Andrew Gaffney
David Gould
Matt Higgins
William J. Hochswender
Alex Hutchinson
Charles Plueddeman
Ty Wenger

FOREWORD *by* ROBERT LIPSYTE

Science bored me in high school and scared me in college. But then around noon on April 16, 1962, in a dank clubhouse at the old Polo Grounds in New York, science suddenly became exciting and relevant. Jay Hook drew a diagram to show me why a curveball curves.

Not that I fully understood. I was a 24-year-old *New York Times* sportswriter and former English major. Hook was a 26-year-old right-handed pitcher for the New York Mets and an engineering graduate of Northwestern University. He was also a member of the American Rocket Society. The intricacies of Bernoulli's law, which he was explaining, were over my head. But Hook was a patient teacher and he was trying to distract himself; that day's game against Houston had been postponed by rain, and Hook would get the chance again the next day to register the very first win for what would be baseball's worst team.

He told me that the principles behind the curveball were the same as those that kept an airplane aloft. He talked about air pressure and boundary layers. "This is really quite simplified," he said apologetically. He was smiling when he said, "Just because you understand Bernoulli's law doesn't mean you can apply it effectively."

Hook was primarily a fastball pitcher, and his own curveball was hittable. He didn't win that next day, but a week later, in Pittsburgh, he did get credit for the first victory in Mets history. By that time, my story about him and Bernoulli, along with his diagram, had appeared and he was known in New York as the thinking fan's pitcher. I got more credit than I deserved for my science erudition.

But my interest was now piqued in the science of sports, which was just beginning to become an aspect of intelligent coverage of athletics. Over the next 40 years, we started writing about atmospheric conditions in yacht racing and the bone structure of racehorses. There were stories about the importance of the spiral to maintain stability in a long pass in football and about brain damage to boxers. The athletic version of the Cold War—the Olympic rivalry between the Soviet Union and the United States—put a spotlight on the emergence of sports medicine, from orthopedic repair to chemical performance enhancement.

I wish I had been more sophisticated about drugs in the 1970s. While I was aware of "greenies," the amphetamines that baseball players popped like candy, it was years before I realized the impact of steroids on football and track-and-field events. I can remember looking at all the "backne," those splashes of pimples on football players' shoulders and backs, and wondering if the equipment was chafing their skin. The few times I asked, I got nasty replies that would now be ascribed to 'roid rage. By the 1980s, most professional and big-time college teams had psychologists, nutritionists, and weight-training specialists, along with more and more doctors with prescription pads. By the 1990s, the technology was NASA-grade, from hand-eye training machines at Olympic prep sites to the heart-and-lung monitors the bike racers wore. Every sportswriter needed to know as much about fast-twitch versus slow-twitch muscles as about the Curse of the Bambino.

Of course, by the 21st century, the Curse was part of the science story. Babe Ruth's single-season and career home-run records were again broken, this time by players suspected of steroid use, and that became the focus of a larger discussion of performance enhancement in sports and in the larger society. Athletes were undergoing Lasik surgery to improve their eyesight, as well as complex regimens of supplements and injections of anesthesia before a game. Why was that different from men using Viagra and opera singers taking beta-blockers to overcome stage fright and school kids being dosed with candy-flavored meds to keep them calm and focused? Weren't steroids, human growth hormone, and EPO logical extensions? Was science leading us into a "post-human" era?

The chance to talk sports with chemists, biologists, physicists, and neurologists was fascinating, but sometimes depressing. Most of this was, after all, junkie science, the search for better ways to cheat through drugs. I yearned for something more positive, another shot of Bernoulli.

Then, around noon on January 14, 2001, in a garage outside Charlotte, North Carolina, I became as excited as I'd been back in the Polo Grounds almost 40 years earlier. I was doing research in preparation for covering NASCAR in my *New York Times* sports column, and a young mechanic, noting my interest, showed me a square piece of aluminum with holes. It was a so-called restrictor plate, placed between the carburetor and the intake manifold to reduce the flow of air and fuel into the engine's combustion chamber. It was used in super-speedway racing to reduce horsepower and speed. It had been mandated for safety, but many drivers thought that because it made passing more difficult, it led to closer racing and more crashes.

For me, it was Bernoulli time again; I didn't understand all the science, but it led me to find out more—about torque, fuel consumption, wind-tunnel testing, and the growing call for head and neck restraints. After covering NASCAR for several years, I wrote a novel for teenagers about stock car racing, *Yellow Flag*, which gave me an excuse to spend even more time in the garage and the pits, talking technology.

I wish I had had some version of this wonderful book to refer to through the past 40 years—enriching games, answering questions. I'm sending a copy to my first successful science teacher, Jay Hook, who went on to pitch in 160 games over eight big-league seasons from 1957 to 1964, winning 29 and losing 62 for the Cincinnati Reds and the Mets. He then went into industry before starting a third career as a professor at Northwestern. Several years ago, after retiring from academia, Jay asked me for a copy of that story I had written about him in 1962; he couldn't find it, and he wanted his grandchildren to know he wasn't just a science geek.

I sent him the story and we laughed about legendary manager Casey Stengel's comment about it, which all sports scientists should keep in mind. When Stengel read the story the next day, he shook his head and said, "If Hook could only do what he knows."

INTRODUCTION

The ancient Greeks and Romans played sports with gusto, and the modern human being is no less an enthusiast. But unlike sporting contests of yore, science and technology now play more prominent roles even in those sports that have seemingly remained unchanged. Behind the thrown ball and churning legs lie such scientific fields as fluid dynamics and biomechanics. Technology is critical for speed in cycling, protection in football, performance measurement in every sport, and so much more.

Why a Curveball Curves is designed for both the player and the fan. The player who understands the science and technology involved in sports is a better-prepared athlete. Likewise, the spectator can grasp more subtle nuances of competition and better appreciate the effort that goes into an individual sport. Here, practitioners of individual sports, whether they are athletes or coaches, examine the science in their game.

Why a Curveball Curves reflects the wide-ranging interest of POPULAR MECHANICS magazine and its editors in many different forms of athletics. Some of the stories have appeared in the magazine, while other essays were written for this book. But if POPULAR MECHANICS can be said to have a favorite sport, it would be baseball, as that game has received the most attention in its pages. The magazine has a long-lasting relationship with Jim Kaat, an ex-major-league pitcher and television broadcaster, who authored a number of essays that appear in this book. Likewise, physics Professor Peter Brancazio of Brooklyn College, author of a book called *Sport Science*, has served the magazine as a longtime scientific advisor regarding the spins and trajectories of baseballs, footballs, basketballs, and moving objects in general.

Other luminaries who have penned their own stories include the clutch football kicker Matt Bahr and baseball legend Lou Piniella. Coaches often offer insights that surpass those of the athlete. Dr. Joe Vigil brings 30 years of experience coaching the marathon, his most famous pupil being Deena Kastor, who won a Bronze Medal in the Athens Olympics in 2004 and continues to rack up distance-running awards around the globe. Likewise, Bob Bowman coached Olympic swimmer Michael Phelps to a trunkful of medals. Jeff Huber served as an Olympic diving coach in both 2000 and 2004. When the seasons change and water turns to ice, veteran skating coach Laura Stamm comes in and gets feet moving faster. These firsthand accounts are supplemented by journalists writing on a range of sports that includes bowling, boxing, hockey, skiing, soccer, and tennis. Equally important are reports on behind-the-scenes trends in training involving vision, hydration, and lactic acid, to name just a few. And a cautionary note is sounded regarding gene doping and its potential to threaten the integrity of all sports, much as illegal drug use did before it.

So, whether you are minutes away from competing as a player or moments away from watching your favorite team, *Why a Curveball Curves* will make you love sports even more—and may even make you a better athlete.

Frank Vizard
Editor

CHAPTER 1

Training

START WITH THE EYES

by STEPHEN A. BOOTH

SEE THE BALL, HIT THE BALL. THAT'S THE MANTRA COUNTLESS YOUNG ATHLETES HAVE HEARD FROM GENERATIONS OF COACHES. ALTHOUGH MOST TRAINING IN SPORTS INVOLVES PHYSICAL REGIMENS LIKE BATTING STANCE, OR MUSCULAR COORDINATION SUCH AS SHIFTING WEIGHT, EXPERTS NOW STRESS THE IMPORTANCE OF EXERCISING AND TRAINING ANOTHER SET OF ORGANS— THE EYES.

Much is made of what's called hand-eye coordination, and while it seems to come naturally to some people, the visual component is teachable and trainable—for adults as well as children. That's the message from authorities such as the American Optometric Association (AOA), as well as optometric specialists at sports training clinics such as the well-regarded Frozen Ropes baseball franchise. Their advice and training techniques can benefit those who play golf, tennis, soccer, hockey, and other sports besides baseball, although most research has focused on the latter.

"How many times have your players just missed catching a ball by inches?" asks Dr. Howard Bailey, a partner in Frozen Ropes' vision-training program. "Remember the great players who were not fleet of foot, but seemed to be in front of the balls hit to them. They got a jump on the ball, or to put it another way, they had fast recognition/release skills."

The body goes into motion only after it receives a visual cue from the eyes to the brain, says Bailey. "If a fielder has an 11.5-second speed in the 100-yard dash, he would gain 27 inches traveling 30 feet by reducing his recognition/release time by 25 percent. Imagine how this training would benefit base stealing, running down fly balls, or any other action that requires moving to a spot to complete a play."

IMPROVE YOUR VISION

Improving one's visual skills for sports begins with a visit to an optometrist for a thorough eye examination, the AOA advises. An optometrist with expertise in sports vision not only can prescribe the right eyeglasses or contact lenses, but also can design a vision therapy program for a specific sport.

There are several components in maximizing vision for sports. These include dynamic visual acuity, or the ability to see objects clearly when you or they are moving quickly. Visual concentration, the ability to screen out distractions and stay focused on a target, is also important. "When you commit an error on an easy ground ball or miss a short putt, it may be that you are distracted by things that are happening around you," the AOA says in its report on vision skills for sports. "Our eyes normally react to anything that happens in our field of vision...spectators, other participants, and even the wind blowing leaves on an overhanging branch."

Eye tracking, the discipline of following objects with minimum head motion, is an ability that helps players stay balanced and react to situations quickly. Eye-hand-body coordination, a term that describes how the hands, feet, and muscles respond to the information gathered through the eyes, affects timing and body control. Visual memory, the ability to process and remember a fast-moving, complex picture of people and things, also aids in fast action. "The athlete with good visual memory always seems to be in the right place at the right time," notes the AOA.

Visualization is another technique that can help your performance, reports the AOA. This involves seeing yourself in your "mind's eye" while your eyes are actually seeing and concentrating on something else, usually the ball. Equally as important as visualization is peripheral vision, which focuses on seeing the action around you. Much of what happens in sports does not happen directly in front of you, so it's important to increase your ability to see action to the side without having to turn your head. Other important functions, which can be learned or can be improved with training, include visual reaction time and depth perception (also called stereo acuity). The former is the speed with which your brain interprets and reacts to an opponent's action—say, in returning a tennis serve. The latter concerns your ability to accurately and quickly judge the distance between you and other objects. If you consistently over- or underestimate the distance to your target, poor depth perception may be at fault.

ADJUSTING YOUR VISUAL MECHANICS

Just as baseball players can make mechanical adjustments to their swing, it's possible to adjust their visual mechanics as well. That's the contention of Tony Abbatine, director of national instruction for the Frozen Rope's Training Centers and the chain's medical advisor on vision. Since 1992, Frozen Ropes' researchers have studied the differences between the visual functions of pro baseball players and the general population, testing some 1,500 major- and minor-league players.

Among other conclusions in Frozen Ropes' white paper on the subject is that pro players have better visual acuity and depth perception than other people. They also have better contrast sensitivity, the ability to track a white ball against the stands or against a cloudy sky. There's more to it, though, than natural ability, according to the researchers. "Although visual acuity, stereo acuity, and contrast sensitivity are important to baseball excellence, they alone are not enough to make a major league player," the researchers concluded. "In order for a player to be successful, he must learn to integrate and master these visual functions while playing in a game."

That means visual memory is important—"an object's representation is stored and its memory recalled for future similar tasks. A superior player must use visual functions to quickly and properly identify the fine details of an object (such as a pitch or a fly ball), in order to produce a mental image of the object and allow for correct identification the next time an identical or similar object is seen. This may be important in recognizing the spin of the ball as it leaves the pitcher's hand or the movement of the pitch as it moves along its initial trajectory."

To that end, Frozen Ropes has developed a vision-training computer program called "Scope and Rope" that's used by professional baseball players as well as the youngsters among its clients. It is composed of two different visual exercises to challenge pitch recognition and visual motility, both of which the company contends are trainable.

A LENS FOR SPORTS

Can contact lenses give you an edge in sports? Athletes like marathon world record holder Paula Radcliffe and baseball player Brian Roberts of the Baltimore Orioles swear by new sports-specific contact lenses called Nike MaxSight made by Bausch & Lomb. The Nike MaxSight lenses, available by prescription, work by filtering glare. An amber-colored lens works best for sports with fast-moving objects like baseball or tennis, while a gray-green lens enhances ground contours for golfers. Similar technology is already available in sunglasses.

TRAINING NOTES

by FRANK VIZARD

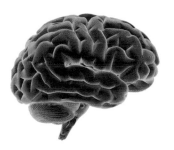

BRAIN OVER PAIN

Pain is all in your head. You might argue against this point the next time you finish a workout and your muscles feel sore. But according to neuroscientists who study the brain, the pain is actually in your head—more specifically, in an area of the cortex called the somatosensory strip. Each part of the body is represented on the strip, and each section on the strip is sized according to its relative sensitivity. Electrical signals from the muscle nerves activate the appropriate section of the strip as a warning signal that the body is overexerting itself. Endomorphins released by the brain block the incoming signals and allow the body to continue to function.

This relationship between the mind and athletic performance is coming under increasing scrutiny by scientists and has been explored in films like IMAX's *Wired to Win: Surviving the Tour de France*. Dr. Martin A. Samuels, a professor of neurology at Harvard Medical School who served as a science advisor on the film, believes that the mind can be used to regulate pain. "You don't need pills to reduce pain," Samuels says. "You can do it inside your head."

Samuels cites the ability of athletes to focus on the activity at hand and put pain in the background. This ability seems to come with training, Samuels says, as initial pain warnings are subsumed with experience gained by repetitive motion. "Muscle memory," as it is sometimes called, is located in the cerebellum rather than in individual muscles. "While clearly there is a genetic capacity that gives us a ceiling we can't go beyond," Samuels says, "hard work and training trumps genetics for most of us. The key to success is in your brain."

LACTIC ACID: YOUR NEW FRIEND

So it turns out lactic acid got a bum rap. For years, lactic acid was condemned as being your worst enemy. Now it turns out to be your best friend.

Anyone who's ever exercised knows what lactic acid is. It's what makes your muscles burn and cramp up. The theory went something like this: Lack of oxygen to the muscles leads to a buildup of lactic acid that leads to muscle fatigue.

Wrong. According to groundbreaking research done in 2006 by Dr. George A. Brooks, a biology professor at the University of California, Berkeley, lactic acid is not a debilitating waste product but a source of fuel. Muscles produce lactic acid from glucose, and they burn it for energy. The lactic acid is used as fuel by mitochondria, the energy-producing power plants inside cells.

So why are you experiencing pain? It's because your muscles haven't learned to burn lactic acid very well. Training helps your muscles convert the lactic acid into fuel more efficiently. In time, the pain goes away as your body adapts. That soreness you experience days later isn't from lactic acid, which dissipates within an hour after you stop exercising. More likely, it's due to minor muscle tears.

Still, despite the mix-up, coaches managed to instruct athletes to do the right thing even if it was for the wrong reasons. Coaches

knew that performances improved when athletes worked on their endurance. As it turns out, endurance training increases the mitochondrial mass, allowing muscles to burn lactic acid better and longer.

As for the scientists, they now know what coaches suspected.

SOLDIERS LOVE KETTLEBELLS

In an age of fancy, high-tech gym equipment, some of the toughest guys in the world are embracing old-fashioned kettlebells as their workout gear of choice. Frontline soldiers in Iraq and Afghanistan, including elite U.S. Navy SEAL teams, are using kettlebells to stay in shape. Developed centuries ago in Russia, kettlebells look like cannonballs with handles, and they come in a range of weights from nine to 106 pounds. And while their portability may make them attractive to soldiers on the move, that's not the reason they're popular. Kettlebells are at the heart of a training regimen based on repetition that makes you strong but bulk-free. Big muscles, it turns out, are less useful in combat where quick movement, speed, agility, and flexibility more often come into play, particularly in rugged, hostile terrain. As one kettlebell-swinging soldier put it, combat is about moving explosively for four to ten feet with what amounts to a small child on your back. What's more, no one on the battlefield asks to see the size of your biceps—strong cores are much more useful for carrying packs and ammo—and you rarely have to bench-press anything. Quick workouts with kettlebells are keeping soldiers at peak strength. The most avid fans of kettlebells enter competitions called Girevoy Sport, after the Russian word for kettleball—*girya*.

TEMPERATURE PILL IS A LIFESAVER

It sounds like something out of a science-fiction film, but for athletes prone to potentially life-threatening attacks of heatstroke and dehydration, their first line of defense may be an ingestible  temperature pill that monitors internal core body temperature and alerts athletic trainers in the event of trouble.

The CorTemp pill, made by HQ Inc. of Palmetto, Florida, is about the size of a multivitamin. An athlete takes the pill a few hours before engaging in an activity, so the pill has time to settle into the lower intestine, where the most stable internal core body temperature readings can be measured. Inside the pill is a temperature-sensitive quartz crystal oscillator, whose vibrations transmit frequencies that are relative to core temperature within the body. Powered by a tiny battery, electronic components transmit the pill's frequencies harmlessly through the body to a handheld data recorder that converts the signal to digital temperature format. The pill stays in the body on average between 24 and 36 hours before being eliminated.

The CorTemp pill is registered with the U.S. Food and Drug Administration (FDA) and works on a low-powered frequency suitable for use in humans. Readings from the pill are easily taken on the sidelines by athletic trainers who hold a data recorder close to the small of an athlete's back. The pill's signal can be transmitted long range up to a 300-foot line-of-sight distance, and multiple athletes can be monitored on a personal digital assistant (PDA) from the sidelines.

The CorTemp pill, which has already been widely adopted in football, where intense summer workouts are common, has been credited with heat-stress interventions even among players who exhibited no symptoms. Pro football and collegiate teams are especially sensitive to this issue after Minnesota Vikings offensive lineman Korey Stringer and University of Florida fullback Eraste Autin died of heatstroke in 2001 during a preseason practice.

The CorTemp ingestible temperature pill is based on technology developed for the National Aeronautics and Space Administration (NASA) to monitor astronauts aboard space shuttles. John Glenn, for example, used one for his return to space at the age of 77 in 1998.

CAN TOO MUCH WATER KILL YOU?

Drink plenty of water to avoid dehydration. That's what athletes have been told for years. But under certain circumstances, that very advice can kill you. The problem is called hyponatremia, a condition that occurs when blood-sodium levels drop dangerously low during intense exercise. If left untreated, hyponatremia can be fatal.

The athletes most susceptible to hyponatremia are those in endurance activities and who are tempted to consume excessive amounts of water or sports drink. Marathon runners clocking slow times of over four hours, for example, are often cited as being vulnerable as they may add four to eight pounds by the end of the race, all of it from fluids. Elite marathon runners may spend less than 30 seconds drinking over a two-hour period. Because the kidneys cannot excrete excess water during intense exercise,

the extra water moves into their cells. This process becomes particularly dangerous when the water moves into brain cells, which have no room to expand. These engorged brain cells press against the skull and compress the brain stem, which controls breathing, with possibly fatal results.

These findings, first reported by the *New England Journal of Medicine*, make the issue of hydration more complex than ever. At the other end of the scale, dehydration can lead to heat exhaustion and heatstroke; the latter is responsible for the deaths of a number of gear-laden football players practicing in late-summer workouts in recent years. Many of those fatalities were among high-school players, and doctors note that the young often do a poor job of keeping themselves hydrated. The American Council on Exercise suggests drinking 8 ounces of water a half hour prior to a 60-minute workout, 4 to 8 ounces every 10 to 15 minutes during exercise, and another 8 ounces within 30 minutes of finishing. This last bit of water intake may be the most important to remember, as studies have shown that players often don't replenish the fluids they've lost before the next practice session begins, thereby increasing their susceptibility to heat injury. Symptoms of heat stress can include pale color, bright red flushing, dizziness, headache, fainting, vomiting, and feeling hot or cold. Changes in performance or personality also are warning signs.

As for marathoners, sip while you run, advise doctors. If you stop to drink a couple of cups, you're drinking too much.

WILL GENE DOPING CREATE A SUPER-ATHLETE?

by FRANK VIZARD

IT STARTED WITH THE IDEA OF DEVELOPING A GENETIC TEST FOR ATHLETES WHO MAY BE SUSCEPTIBLE TO HYPERTROPHIC CARDIOMYOPATHY (HCM), A POTENTIALLY DEADLY HARDENING OF THE WALLS OF THE HEART THAT IS RESPONSIBLE FOR AS MANY AS ONE-THIRD OF SUDDEN-DEATH CASES AMONG ATHLETES UNDER 35. THEN CAME THE LAW OF UNINTENDED CONSEQUENCES COMMONLY REFERRED TO AS "BLOWBACK." THE LEAP FROM A DNA TEST FOR HCM TO A GENETIC TEST THAT MIGHT INDICATE ATHLETIC POTENTIAL IN A SPECIFIED SPORT WAS A SHORT ONE.

Genetic Technologies Corporation, based in Australia, now offers, for a small fee, a genetic test for the *ACTN3* gene that encodes a protein found in fast-twitching muscle fibers crucial to sprinters and other power athletes. Conversely, the presence of two copies of an *ACTN3* mutation called *R577X* means the protein is not produced, perhaps indicating that endurance-oriented sports may be a better calling for the athlete being tested. Other researchers link a gene associated with angiotensin converting enzyme (ACE) to endurance abilities.

Whether testing for the presence of a particular gene proves effective remains to be seen. But in the short term, the presence or lack of *ACTN3* and any other sports-related genes that will be discovered will certainly be among the data that coaches use in training athletes, particularly those at elite levels where even the smallest edge can be the difference between winning and losing.

GENETIC MANIPULATION

The real test may come when DNA testing is harnessed to gene therapy to produce athletes whose abilities are enhanced to their highest degree. The World Anti-Doping Agency (WADA) has already placed such gene doping on its list of prohibited substances and methods, even before any evidence of its existence. With gene manipulation already being done in animals, the worry is that a genetically enhanced super-athlete who is able to run faster, jump higher, and throw farther is not far behind. WADA views gene doping as an inevitability to be practiced by unscrupulous labs of the BALCO (Bay Area Laboratory Cooperative) variety that rocked Major League Baseball by supplying illegal steroids to players.

Most misused drugs in sports are originally created to treat diseases and are considered groundbreaking when developed. Gene therapy represents a giant step forward in the treatment of illnesses, but gene doping could also threaten the integrity of all sports.

Gene doping is simple in theory and not beyond the ability of many of the well-trained people in labs all over the world, noted Dr. Theodore Freidmann, chairman of a WADA panel on gene doping, in a 2005 interview. The technology is evolving very rapidly. Scientists have already experimented with genes that produce insulin-growth factor (IGF-1) to help muscles grow and repair themselves. In these experiments genes are injected using a harmless virus as a carrier. The virus penetrates the cell and delivers its genetic payload. The added genes allow the body to produce more IGF-1 than it would normally, thereby speeding the healing of damaged muscles or strengthening weakened knees and other joints.

For athletes already injecting EPO (Erythropoietin) to enhance performance, gene doping would be the next logical step. Instead of injecting EPO, they would inject themselves with the gene that would allow the body to naturally produce more oxygen-carrying red blood cells to increase muscle endurance.

THE RISKS OF GENE DOPING

Gene doping is not without difficulties and risks. Newly inserted genes have to be able to produce the right amount of extra product at the right time to be effective. For example, after undergoing gene therapy, some French boys suffering from an extreme immune deficiency developed leukemia because the delivery system used

Canadian sprinter Ben Johnson, a two-time Bronze Medal winner in the 1984 Olympics, won the Gold Medal for the 100-meter dash in the 1988 Olympics. After the win, he tested positive for steroids, and his Gold Medal and Olympic title were rescinded.

to target the human cells was about as precise as a shotgun and adversely affected nontargeted cells. And unlike drugs that can be washed out of the body, gene doping can permanently alter the body's cellular structure and may have consequences that don't become evident for years.

TESTING FOR GENE DOPING

From WADA's perspective, the question now is whether gene doping can be detected. The organization already has a half-dozen research projects under way that use a variety of methodologies. One approach is to measure the effect of gene doping on red blood cells just as is done in drug testing. Another approach is to examine the effect of newly added genes on other nearby genes in the hope that an overall pattern or signature can be detected when gene doping occurs. Researchers also think full body scans like those used in magnetic resonance imaging can be developed to search for unusual genetic manifestations.

Whether gene doping can alter the competitive balance in sports remains to be seen, but if the history surrounding drug doping is any indicator, some unscrupulous athlete or lab is soon likely to embrace the possibility of a competitive advantage offered by gene doping.

DRUGS AND THEIR ABUSES

AMPHETAMINES: Commonly used as a stimulant in the treatment of attention-deficit disorder, Parkinson's disease, and narcolepsy. Some athletes take them to build muscle mass, increase endurance, recover more quickly from injury, and stay awake. Long-term abuse includes a weakened immune system, heart problems, and liver, kidney, and lung damage.

ANDROSTENEDIONE: "Andro" is an anabolic steroid that boosts the production of testosterone to build body mass and improve strength and endurance. Side effects in women are development of male characteristics (deepened voice and male-pattern baldness); in men, diminished sperm production, shrinkage of testicles, and enlargement of breasts; for both genders, an increased risk of heart attack or stroke from a lowering of "good" HDL cholesterol.

DARBEPOETIN: Used to treat kidney failure and cancer patients in chemotherapy. This peptide hormone boosts production of red blood cells that carry oxygen to the muscles, thereby increasing endurance levels. The most frequently reported serious adverse reactions are thrombosis, heart failure, sepsis, and cardiac arrhythmia.

>>>

DEHYDROEPIANDROSTERONE:
DHEA is an anabolic agent used to treat a wide variety of illnesses ranging from cardiovascular disease to obesity. Some athletes use it to reduce body fat and promote muscle growth. Side effects may include stunted growth in teens, palpitations, extensive growth of body hair, hair loss, and liver damage.

DIURETICS: Used in weight-reduction programs. Athletes take these masking agents to flush steroids from their systems because the drug increases urine production. Side effects may include palpitations, muscle cramps and weakness, incontinence, kidney damage, and impaired hearing.

EPHEDRINE: Found in cold and allergy medicines, ephedrine is a stimulant that makes the heart beat faster, used to reduce fatigue and boost performance during short bursts of effort. Adverse reactions include dizziness, gastrointestinal distress, chest pain, seizures, and heatstroke.

ERYTHROPOIETIN: EPO is a peptide hormone used to boost the red blood cell count of cancer and AIDS patients. In an athlete, this synthetic version of a naturally occurring hormone increases aerobic capacity and muscle endurance. It also causes circulatory strain as well as clotting in smaller blood vessels.

HUMAN GROWTH HORMONE:
This peptide hormone is used to help stunted children grow normally. Athletes can use it to build muscles, reduce body fat, and recover faster from strenuous workouts. Side effects may include arthritis-like symptoms, diabetes, abnormal growth of bones and internal organs, hardening of the arteries, and high blood pressure.

INSULIN: Diabetics use insulin to control blood-sugar levels, but athletes can use it in conjunction with steroids to build muscle and increase endurance and stamina. Possible side effects include weight gain, hypoglycemia, and sudden drops in blood sugar that can lead to a potentially fatal coma.

METHAMPHETAMINE:
Used to treat obesity and attention-deficit disorder, "speed" can increase an athlete's level of alertness.

Side effects can include high blood pressure, damage to blood vessels in the brain, hyperthermia, hypertension, and cardiovascular collapse.

MODAFINIL: Used to treat narcolepsy, it can also be used to increase alertness. Side effects may include depression, loss of muscle strength, lung problems, amnesia, and asthma.

NANDROLONE: An anabolic agent used to treat wasting diseases and build muscle mass in HIV-infected patients, it can also be used to increase muscle mass and strength in athletes. It occurs naturally but only in tiny quantities. Side effects may include liver damage, sterility, baldness, breast enlargement in men, and male characteristics in women.

NORANDROSTERONE: Found in nutritional supplements, it can be used to build muscle mass and increase strength. Side effects may include liver damage, sterility, baldness, breast enlargement in men, and male characteristics in women.

STANOZOLOL: Used to treat an episodic swelling condition called hereditary angioedema, it can also be used to increase strength and recover more quickly from workouts. Side effects may include liver damage, sterility, baldness, breast enlargement in men, and male characteristics in women.

TESTOSTERONE: Used in the treatment of conditions ranging from impotence to HIV, synthetic versions of the male sex hormone increase strength and muscle mass in athletes. Side effects may include liver damage, sterility, high blood pressure, shrinkage of testicles, enlarged prostate, breast enlargement in men, and male characteristics in women.

TETRAHYDROGESTRINONE: Nicknamed "The Clear," THG is a synthetic anabolic steroid that helps build body mass and improves strength and endurance; side effects are the same as synthetic testosterone. Unlike other anabolic steroids, which are pharmaceuticals intended for veterinary or human use, THG has never been approved for any medical indication.

TOP TEN DOPING SCANDALS

[1] **EAST GERMANY:** An Olympic powerhouse in the 1970s and 1980s, the former Communist nation doubled its Gold Medal count from 20 to 40 in just four years. After the fall of the Berlin Wall, it was revealed that athletes often were unknowingly doped starting as young as thirteen.

[2] **1983 PAN-AMERICAN GAMES:** A surprise test for steroid use nailed American triple Gold Medal winner Jeff Michaels as well as other weightlifters. Michaels was stripped of his medals. Dozens of other athletes withdrew from the competition, heralding the modern age of drug testing.

[3] **THE BALCO AFFAIR:** In 2003, an anonymous track-and-field coach leaked the names of athletes using the steroid THG and provided a used syringe to the U. S. Anti-Doping Administration (USADA). The leak led to the BALCO affair, the conspiracy to provide previously undetectable steroids to athletes in many sports, most notably in baseball and track-and-field events. Top athletes fell under suspicion, and some were suspended from their sports when urine samples were found to have traces of THG.

[4] **TOUR DE FRANCE:** The world's most famous bicycle race has been tarnished by the seemingly never-ending association of riders with performance-enhancing drugs in 1998, 2002, 2004, 2006, and 2007.

>>>

[5] **BEN JOHNSON:** The Canadian sprinter narrowly edged out Carl Lewis in the 100-meter dash for the Gold Medal in the 1988 Seoul Olympics but then tested positive for steroids, heightening concern about the use of drugs in sports. Johnson was disqualified.

[6] **BASEBALL'S HOME-RUN HITTERS:** Mark McGwire admitted to the then-legal use of andro after breaking the single-season home-run record in 1998, while Barry Bonds passed Hank Aaron on the all-time list under a cloud of suspicion that pervades the sport. Baseball is called the new East Germany.

[7] **CHINA'S SWIMMERS:** Since 1990, 40 Chinese swimmers have failed drug tests, triple the number of any other country.

[8] **THE WHISKEY TEST:** Irish swimmer Michelle Smith came out of nowhere to win three Gold Medals and one Silver Medal in the 1996 Atlanta Olympics while also managing to evade drug testers. Caught at home in a surprise test, Smith used alcohol to tamper with her urine sample and got a four-year suspension.

[9] **CROSS-COUNTRY SKIING:** EPO and steroids joined ski wax in the kits of competitors in the 2001 World Nordic Championships and at the 2002 Salt Lake Olympics, where several athletes tested positive for banned substances and were stripped of their medals.

[10] **NANDROLONE:** By 2005, it achieved status as the most widely used steroid in athletics, but its use may be inadvertent as it is found in improperly labeled diet supplements, energy drinks, and vitamins.

Baseball

BASEBALL IS A HITTER'S GAME

by JIM KAAT

This article appeared in
POPULAR MECHANICS in 2003.

CRITICS OF BASEBALL
WILL TELL YOU THAT
ABNER DOUBLEDAY
OF COOPERSTOWN,
NEW YORK, INVENTED
THE GAME IN 1839
AND NOT A THING
HAS CHANGED SINCE.
NOTHING COULD BE
FURTHER FROM THE
TRUTH. BACK THEN,
IT WAS A PITCHER'S
GAME. TODAY, IT'S
THE HITTER WHO IS
IN CONTROL.

THE CHANGING GAME

First, no one has yet proved that Ol' Abner actually invented the game, and second, the game of baseball constantly changes—with every game, every day, and every player bringing something unique to the sport. The peanuts and Cracker Jack are still there, but everything else is different than it was even five years ago. In my opinion, no sport has changed as radically as baseball in the past twenty years. To me, baseball is a matter of who's in control—the pitcher or the hitter. The vast majority of the changes in Major League Baseball over the past twenty years have favored putting the hitter in control. Why? Because fans would rather see an 11–8 ball game with balls getting smacked over the fence than a 2–1 pitcher's duel. And hitters today are delivering.

Players are bigger and more durable than in years past. Take Toronto's Troy Glaus, for example. This guy is 6-foot 5, 240 pounds, and quick on his feet. It's a matter of simple physics that a stronger player is going to hit the ball farther. And hitters have been doing it with regularity.

Today, many of the pitcher's weapons have been taken away. The legendary Roger Clemens and a few other old-school power pitchers make their money pitching inside. That sets up low and away, which is the most difficult pitch to reach with the fat of the bat. Throwing high and inside makes a hitter feel uncomfortable and keeps him from diving in. That makes the outside corner fertile territory.

While no rules exist as to how close a hitter can crowd the plate, the current situation borders on the ridiculous. Today, either the grounds crew doesn't line the inside of the batter's box at all or the first few hitters scratch it out with their foot. So you'll see the Yankees' Derek Jeter or the Giants' Barry Bonds right on top of the plate with their front arm hanging into the strike zone. They no longer fear the inside pitch. And why should they? Consider all the protective gear batters are allowed to wear today—wrist guards, forearm protectors, elbow protectors, gloves, and double-flap batting helmets.

Then there are the knockdown rules. Can you imagine a guy hanging right over the plate in the old days with someone like the

Derek Jeter of the New York Yankees is a lifetime .300 hitter.

Cardinals' Bob Gibson or the Dodgers' Don Drysdale on the mound? As soon as a guy leaned over into the strike zone, the first pitch from one of those pitchers was a blazing fastball high and inside. Today, a pitcher can't push a hitter off the plate because of the knockdown rules in effect. If you do throw one up and in and the umpire deems that you threw it there intentionally, there's a warning. A second close pitch gets you thrown out of the game. It's in the written rules. So that takes away the inside pitch immediately.

THE SHRINKING STRIKE ZONE

In 1963, the strike zone was defined in the rules as the width of home plate horizontally, extending vertically from the batter's letters down to the bottom of the knee. In 1969, it was changed to the bottom of the armpit down to the top of the knee. In the rule book, that's still the strike zone. But today, umpires are allowed to "interpret" the strike zone as they see fit in any given game. Thus, on one hand, you see strikes being called that are well off the plate. On the other hand, when was the last time you saw a strike being called on any pitch higher than the batter's belt? It just doesn't happen.

The 1968 season was the one that started the shrinking process. It has been called the "year of the pitcher." St. Louis's Bob Gibson had a monster year, winning 22 of 31 games, carving out a 1.12 ERA, striking out 268 batters, and pitching thirteen shutouts. If pitchers were hot, batters were not. Carl Yastrzemski of the Boston Red Sox led the American League in batting with a paltry .301 average. Baseball moguls feared diminishing fan interest in low-scoring games and felt they needed more excitement in the game—which translated into more offense. Since then, most rule changes have favored batters.

Television has given baseball an opportunity to review an umpire's performance and determine how many pitches he missed—or called correctly. The pitch missed most often is on the low outside corner. That's due, in part, to the umpire's inside chest protector, which has replaced the old, cumbersome inflatable protectors. Simply put, the inside protector is

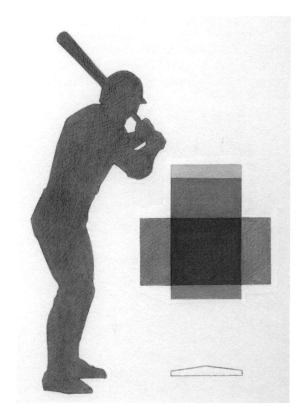

Smaller Strike Zone: Once stretching from the letters to below the knee, it is now recognized from the armpit to above the knee. Umpires tend to call an even shorter, wider zone.

less bulky but doesn't protect as well. Nowadays, you don't see umps squaring up right behind the catcher, which would allow them to see both corners. Instead, umpires peek over the inside corner. Why the inside corner? Because if a ball is fouled off, it's almost always toward the outside. The umpire doesn't want to get hit with a foul ball. They hurt. So he stays inside. Better for the ump, but it makes for a lot more guesswork in the outside pitch.

THE LOWER PITCHER'S MOUND

In 1969, Major League Baseball lowered the pitcher's mound from fifteen inches to ten inches. The higher you can get on the mound and look down on the hitter, the more leverage you have and the more that ball is coming from twelve o'clock to six o'clock. That makes it more difficult to hit the ball squarely compared to pitches coming in on a flat plane. Again, another advantage now for the hitter.

Lower Pitcher's Mound: A lower mound puts pitchers at a disadvantage.

SMALLER BALLPARKS

With just about everything else in baseball shrinking except players' salaries, it's no surprise that most of the newer ballparks are smaller than the ones they replace. Take Yankee Stadium. In the original ballpark, the distance to hit one out in center field was an unbelievable 487 feet. Left-center wasn't called Death Valley for nothing. You had to slam it 500 feet to reach the stands. The new stadium, remodeled in 1988, has left-center at 399 feet and center field at 408 feet. Still healthy shots, but nothing like it was. Poor Joe DiMaggio. He hit many a tremendous shot to left-center or center at the old stadium, and they were mere fly balls. Yet the short 295-foot distance down the right-field foul line (314 feet today) was tailor-made for the likes of the left-hand-hitting Babe Ruth and, in recent times, Mickey Mantle (when he batted left), Reggie Jackson, Bobby Murcer, and Jason Giambi. Today, a season barely goes by without a Sosa, Bonds, or Rodriguez hitting 50, 60, even 70 home runs. No wonder.

Smaller Stadiums: Yankee Stadium has shrunk since it originally opened in 1923. Center field and the power alleys are reduced. A shorter center field plays to a batter's ability to hit straightaway. Yet foul-pole distances have increased, putting pull hitters, who tend to hit to the same side of the field that they bat, at a disadvantage.

BATS, BALLS, AND SURFACES

Speaking of hitting home runs, Major League Baseball contends that ball specs are the same as they've always been. But players

The lighter, harder maple Sam Bat springs back more quickly after making contact with the ball.

believe that the ball is harder and unquestionably livelier. I personally believe—and so do a lot of current players—that the ball today is livelier than it was ten years ago. Couple that with the new bats, which reflect a much more significant change, and hitters have yet another big advantage. Bats traditionally have been made of ash, which is a less dense wood than maple. Ash is porous and absorbs moisture. Years ago, hitters I played with, such as Mantle or Harmon Killebrew, wouldn't swing a bat that weighed less than 34 to 35 ounces. The Canadian-made Sam Bat used by Barry Bonds weighs just 30 ounces, has a very thin handle, and is made of sugar maple. It is kiln-dried down to a 7 to 9 percent moisture content and then varnished. Drier, harder bats give you a higher coefficient of restitution. In other words, they spring back more quickly after making contact with the ball. This, combined with higher bat speeds and the livelier ball, means the ball jumps off the bat faster and travels farther. More home runs.

Did you know that the artificial turf and "hard" natural grass found in today's ballparks give hitters yet another advantage over pitchers? They do. When hit on the ground, the ball travels much more quickly through the infield. More balls go through for hits because the infielders simply can't get to the ball in time. Batting averages go up, more runs are scored, and the fans cheer.

ATHLETE FITNESS AND CARE

Then there is the health and fitness question. It's better. No question. Years ago, a trainer was kind of an all-purpose guy who handed out vitamins and salt pills, and he had a can of ethyl chloride to temporarily freeze an area to kill pain if you got hit with a ball. Trainers today are much better qualified, and they have all kinds of special equipment to treat just about everything. Massage therapists, common today, were unheard of in the old days. And the list of bodybuilding supplements today—both legal and questionable—is almost endless.

With weight training and exercise regimens, players are stronger and more durable. Stretching exercises and equipment are used every day to prevent as well as treat injuries. Another thing: Nobody looks at you funny if you spend some time in the whirlpool. The old saying used to be, "You can't make the club in the tub."

Sports surgery is another area that's really come a long way, and it directly impacts player durability and longevity. Years ago, surgeons would try to keep a player's muscles together with staples, and that just about ended many careers. With the new arthroscopic techniques, a surgeon can repair a guy's knee or elbow, and the player can be back on the active roster in weeks. All this adds up to hitters who are bigger, stronger, more durable, and hit the ball a ton—like that Troy Glaus guy I mentioned at the beginning.

Expansion has seen Major League Baseball go from sixteen teams to 30 teams over the past 40 years. Is it any wonder that pitching talent is scarce and getting scarcer? There simply aren't enough good pitchers to go around. Which is great if you're a hitter.

In the old days, it was common for the best all-around athlete to be a pitcher. It was a prestigious position. After all, nothing happened until he threw the ball. I was very proud to be a major-league pitcher. But if I had to do it all over again today, I'd probably want to be a hitter. That's where the glory is now.

HOW BASEBALL HAS CHANGED SINCE THE 1920S
by DAVIN COBURN

Here are four ways baseball has evolved since the 1920s:

[1] **BIGGER GUNS:** Weight training and performance-enhancing drugs have helped out at the plate, though there's no telling how widely drug use has permeated the game. According to baseball-reference.com, there were 1.12 homers per game in the 2001 season—three times more than in 1927.

[2] **BETTER BALLS:** You can't hit what you can't see. Until 1920, baseballs often were covered in tobacco juice. Then Cleveland Indians shortstop Ray Chapman was killed by a pitch thrown by New York Yankees hurler Carl Mays on August 16, 1920; the spitball was replaced by clean, white balls, and home runs took off.

[3] **SLICKER PITCHES:** These days, cut fastballs, split-fingers, and sliders keep hitters off their heels. The year 2001 saw 6.67 strikeouts per game—almost 2.5 times more than in 1927.

[4] **SMALLER ZONES:** With a 17-inch-wide plate, a 6-foot-2-inch player in 1927, like Babe Ruth, had a strike zone of roughly 545 square inches. By 2001, rule changes shrank the zone of a 6-foot-2-inch player, like Barry Bonds, to about 410 square inches.

ANATOMY OF
A SWING

by DAVIN COBURN

IN LESS TIME THAN IT TAKES TO BLINK, PRO HITTERS ROUTINELY ACHIEVE THE EXTRAORDINARY.

When Ryan Zimmerman stands at the plate, there's no time to analyze physics. "I'm thinking about what the pitcher might throw in that situation," says the 22-year-old rising star with the Washington Nationals. "I have to eliminate as many options as I can before he releases the ball." Twenty times in the 2006 season, Zimmerman pounded a pitch into the seats. Let's stop the clock to examine ball spin, bat speed, and the rest of what Zimmerman instinctively understands about hitting. Here's how those home runs happened.

SPIN CONTROL

A fastball comes to the plate with backspin—up to 1,800 revolutions per minute (rpm). To hit the ball out of the park, a batter must reverse the rotation of the ball so that it leaves the bat with backspin. This gives the ball lift.

A curveball can carry topspin of 1,900 rpm, making it bite downward as it crosses the plate. By crushing a curve, a batter builds on the pitcher's topspin—producing 45 percent more backspin off the bat.

The result? Curveballs can be hit farther. Mont Hubbard of the University of California, Davis, found that a 94-mile-per-hour (mph) fastball leaves the bat 3 mph faster than a 78-mph curveball—but it travels 442 feet compared to the curve's 455 feet.

BAT SPEED VERSUS MASS

Boosting two factors—the mass of the bat and the speed of the swing—can raise batted ball speed (BBS), which adds distance to a hit. But swing speed can affect BBS more dramatically.

Research has shown that doubling the weight of a 20-ounce wood bat can raise BBS of 68.5 mph to 80.4 mph—a 17.3 percent increase. But Daniel Russell, a professor at Kettering University in Michigan, found that doubling the swing speed of a 30-ounce bat can raise a BBS of 62 mph to 83.8 mph—a 35.1 percent increase.

In terms of turning a hit into a homer: against a 94-mph fastball, every 1-mph increase in swing speed extends distance about 8 feet.

Ryan Zimmerman, third baseman for the Washington Nationals, at bat against the Colorado Rockies at RFK Stadium, in Washington, D.C., in June 2006. The Nationals fell to the Rockies 4–3 in the first game of the four-game series.

THE IDEAL BAT

University of Arizona professor Terry Bahill found that the maximum bat weight before swing speed drops is about 41 ounces. But a pro player's ideal bat weight, he says, is lighter—in the 31- to 32-ounce range. This weight produces a BBS 1 percent below the BBS of the maximum-weight bat—allowing the batter greater maneuverability with a negligible loss of power.

Zimmerman has discovered the same principle with his 34-inch, 32-ounce MaxBat. "A bigger bat obviously has more solid wood," he says, "but you can handle a smaller bat better."

FORCING THE ISSUE

Major-league baseballs have an average mass of 5.125 ounces, and a 90-mph fastball can leave the bat at 110 mph. Extrapolating Newton's second law of motion, Russell determined that, in a collision lasting less than one-thousandth of a second, the average pro swing imparts 4,145 pounds of force to the ball. Peak forces exceed 8,300 pounds—enough to stop a Mini Cooper, rolling at 10 mph, in its tracks.

MAXING OUT

Contrary to the lore surrounding historic, titanic blasts—like Mickey Mantle's fabled 565-foot shot in 1953—physicists estimate that the farthest a man can hit a ball, at sea level, without help from the wind, is about 475 feet.

A SUPERSIZE SWEET SPOT

A bat vibrates at multiple frequencies when it collides with a ball. How much energy is transferred to the ball—instead of spread through the bat and the batter's hands—depends on where the collision occurs. A bat vibrating at its fundamental frequency (below, in black) has a node of zero vibration about 6^1/$_2$ inches from the barrel end (Node 1). This was long thought to be the bat's sweet spot. But Rod Cross, a physicist at Australia's University of Sydney, found that the spot is more like a zone. At a second frequency (in red), a bat has another node about 4^1/$_2$ inches down the barrel (Node 2). Hits between the two produce minimal vibration—and transfer more energy—at both frequencies. "Every ball I've hit that I haven't felt, I knew I hit well," Zimmerman says.

Washington Nationals third baseman Ryan Zimmerman hit .287 with 20 homers and 110 RBIs in 2006. He finished second in the National League Rookie of the Year voting.

THINKING QUICKLY

A 90-mph fastball can reach home plate in 400 milliseconds—or four-tenths of a second. But a batter has just a quarter-second to identify the pitch, decide whether to swing, and start the process. "Once the pitch is in flight, it's the snap of your fingers," Zimmerman says. What happens next is "pretty much just instinct." A batter takes 100 milliseconds to see the three-inch ball, and 75 milliseconds to identify spin, speed, and pitch location. The batter has another 50 milliseconds to decide whether to swing, and where, before he must act. It can take nearly 25 milliseconds for the brain's signals to pulse through the hitter's body and start his legs moving. The swing itself takes 150 milliseconds.

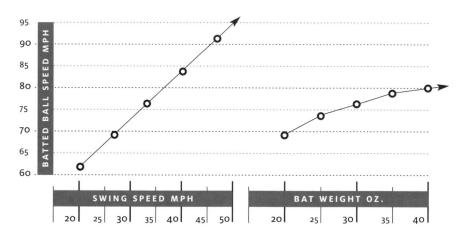

For the first 50 milliseconds of a swing, a batter can stop his two-pound bat in time to check the swing. By 110 milliseconds, the bat, moving at up to 80 mph, carries too much inertia to be stopped.

HOW TO HIT
A HOMER

by LOU PINIELLA

This article appeared in
POPULAR MECHANICS in 1991.

THE HOME RUN CAN WIN A BALL GAME FOR YOU WITH ONE SWING OF THE BAT. NO QUESTION. IT'S THE MOST EXCITING HIT IN BASEBALL. BY EXTENSION, THE GUYS WHO CAN SMASH A BASEBALL 400 FEET OR MORE OVER A FENCE ARE AMONG THE MOST EXCITING PLAYERS IN THE GAME.

How far can a baseball be hit? The old-timers talk about Mickey Mantle hitting one 565 feet. I've seen some audacious shots but never one in the 500-foot category. I'd say 450 to 475 feet is about as far as a human being can hit a baseball without help from the elements.

HITTING THEORIES

There are basically two schools of thought when it comes to hitting a baseball. One was developed by Ted Williams, the legendary Boston Red Sox slugger. The Williams school emphasizes a rotation of the hips to generate power.

The second school of thought is best articulated by Charley Lau, a former coach with the Kansas City Royals, New York Yankees, and others. The Lau school puts a premium on making contact with the ball. Lau asks you to keep your head down and shift your weight from back to front as you swing.

While Ted Williams was my idol as a child, I'm philosophically more in the Charley Lau school. If you throw your hips as Williams recommends, your hands are going to drag, and your swing is going to be a little longer. Your navel is going to lead, and your hands are going to catch up a little late.

With the Williams approach, it is much easier to hit the low ball. On the low pitch, you have more time to catch up to the ball. The higher a pitch is in the strike zone, the harder it is to catch up to it. Your swing has to be shorter and more compact.

The problem is that as the ball moves up the strike zone, it will hop a little more and have two to three miles per hour more velocity.

The hitting method I'm going to describe is fundamentally derived from the Lau school, but with a variation designed to deliver more power. Does it work? When Chris Sabo of the Cincinnati Reds used this approach, he upped his home-run production from 6 to 25 homers in a year.

STANCE

What you want in your stance is balance. Balance allows you to do a lot of things. It allows you to get a good weight shift. It allows

Ryan Howard of the Philadelphia Phillies hit 58 home runs in 2006, his third season in the major leagues.

you to go out after a breaking ball. It allows you to wait on an off-speed pitch.

The way George Brett of the Kansas City Royals stood in the batter's box was nice to see. The good hitter will lean forward across the plate and then shift his weight back. One way to set your balance in this manner is to reach across the plate with your bat. I used to do this every at bat. It was a great balancing trick for me. Brett did this also. He leaned out, touched the other side of the plate, and then he was ready to hit a baseball. He knew exactly how much extension he needed to the outside of the plate.

In terms of positioning the feet, the home-run hitter cannot have a very closed stance—meaning one in which the front leg is closer to the plate than the back leg. Most of the guys hitting the ball out of the park have a slightly open or square stance. This means the front leg is a degree or two off a straight line that can be

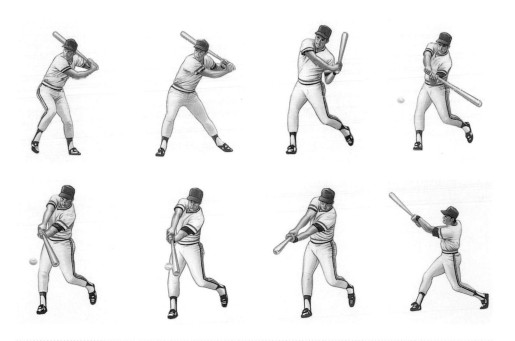

Home-run hitters use a front-knee cock to get their weight back. The front knee acts like a trigger and also gets the batter's hands back. As the ball enters the hitting zone, the hands lead the body through the swing. The bottom hand provides the extension needed to cover the plate and supplies power. The top hand guides the bat. After contact is made, the hands grip the bat in the follow-through. This produces a total weight shift that helps generate the power needed to hit the ball out of the park.

drawn from the back leg of the batter to the pitcher. Even if they start out slightly closed, they all wind up slightly open when they're done.

Home-run hitters don't have very wide stances. Most stances are about a shoulder width—a position that allows them to stride and make good use of the weight transfer in their lower bodies when they swing.

Once you're in the batter's box, don't lock into a stance. There should be a little movement in the feet. Like a tennis player awaiting a serve, your feet should not be stationary. If a tennis player can return a fast-moving ball, that tells me you can get set to swing off movement more quickly than you can from a stationary position.

BODY MOVEMENT

All home-run hitters have one thing in common—the front-knee cock. It's really their trigger to get everything going. When the knee cocks, you're shifting weight to the back leg and getting ready to drive off it. In baseball, you have to go back before you can go forward. As the knee is cocked, you can get a small turn at the hip and at the shoulder. This turning motion helps the hitter get his hands back.

At this point, the great home-run hitters do something you can't teach. Amazingly, most of your home-run hitters don't have a classic swing. Most of them have hitches—a little up-down motion with the bat at the start of their swing that's just innate. Hitch or no hitch, at this point there should be a straight line coming up from your back foot through your hip to the top of your back shoulder.

Your shoulders should be fairly horizontal at the start of the swing, but as you make contact, the front shoulder is going to be a little higher than your back shoulder. This is because there is no such thing as a level swing. Everyone swings slightly up. Home-run hitters swing slightly more up than other hitters. The higher up you finish, the more power you get—not to mention lift.

BAT GRIP AND WEIGHT SHIFT

The bat should be held in a relaxed, loose grip. Somebody should be able to pull it out of your hands. The bottom hand should grip the bat a little more tightly than at the top. The bottom hand is the lead hand because this hand gives you the extension.

All home-run hitters get bottom-hand extension. That's what gives them power. Everyone thinks the top hand gives you power, but the bottom hand provides most of it. The top hand steers the

Some pitches are more likely to be hit out for home runs than others. Baseball people always tell pitchers to "keep it low." The truth is most home runs come on down-and-in fastballs and breaking balls that let hitters fully extend. More home runs are hit when the ball is in the red zone. The orange zone is number two and the yellow zone is number three. It becomes progressively more difficult to hit a home run when the ball is in the green, blue, and purple zones. The blue zone jumps to the number one spot for hanging breaking balls.

bat. If the top hand dominates the swing, the bat will be in and out of the hitting area very quickly. With bottom-hand extension, you stay in the hitting area much longer.

Now, here's where I disagree with Lau and his disciples. They suggest bottom-hand extension, but with top-hand release of the bat upon contact. I don't agree with that because you lose power. You're not getting the back side of your body to drive through the ball.

If you look at your home-run hitter, there isn't one who lets the top hand go off the bat. The bottom hand gets the hitter to the ball. The top hand gets the hitter through the ball. By holding on to the bat with both hands into the follow-through, you get a total weight shift that delivers more power into the swing.

You let go of the bat only when you've driven all the way through the ball—when it's no longer physically possible to hold on to the bat because the bottom hand has extended well beyond the top hand's ability to hang on. At this point, your back foot is slightly off the ground or has pivoted so only the toe is touching the dirt.

With the Lau method, you get a pretty good lateral weight shift, but not a total weight shift. Without a total weight shift, you can't generate the power to drive the ball out of the park as consistently. With Lau, the front foot may skate forward a little and the top hand leaves the bat upon contact. There is no trigger or top-hand follow-through to generate a total weight shift for power hitting. Likewise, I disagree with the Williams method of throwing the hips at the ball. I believe in throwing the hands at the ball and letting the hips follow the hands.

Technique helps a lot, of course, but a lot of what constitutes a home-run hitter occurs naturally. There's the hitch, for one thing. Home-run hitters also go to the ball more quickly. They don't take a long time deciding on whether or not to swing.

For the most part, home-run hitters use a bat that is two to three ounces heavier than most, with a thinly tapered handle and lots of barrel on the end. It takes a man to swing it. Home-run hitters want a club to slug the ball. When they connect properly, the ball is as likely to go out of the park as it is anywhere else.

BABE RUTH'S HOME-RUN SECRETS

by A. A. ALBELLI

The famed New York Yankees slugger Babe Ruth (1895–1948) hit 714 home runs during a career that ended in 1935. Ruth's record stood until Hank Aaron of the Atlanta Braves broke it in 1974. This article appeared in POPULAR MECHANICS in 1928.

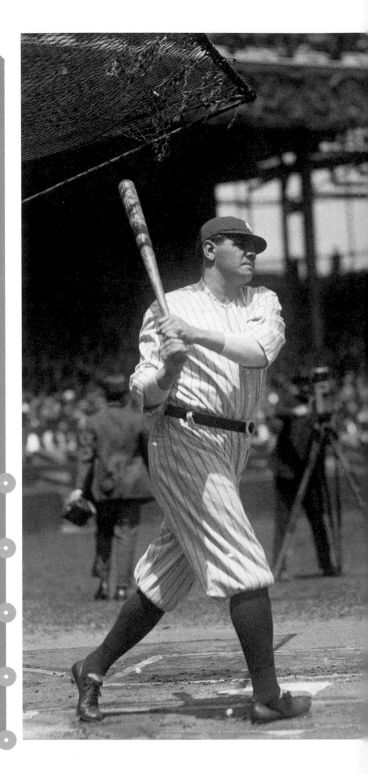

THAT STODGY URCHIN WHO USED TO CATCH FOR A SCHOOL BASEBALL TEAM YEARS AGO, NOW GROWN TO BE THE GREATEST FIGURE EVER KNOWN TO THE SPORT, TOLD ME THE OTHER DAY THAT HE EXPECTS TO CLOUT 100 HOME RUNS FOR THE NEW YORK YANKEES NEXT SEASON.

Babe Ruth at bat in New York: the Yankees vs. St. Louis at the Polo Grounds on May 20, 1922.

There is nothing of the braggadocio about Babe Ruth. He is all that baseball-loving America looks for in its idol. The halo which popularity has woven about him has not changed his boyish personality.

"The way I have come to feel," he said, "I can knock out 100 homers any old season from now on." During the 1927 season, he reached the record of 60 circuit drives. He added two more when the Yankees played the Pittsburgh Pirates in the World Series.

"The only thing that will prevent me from slamming out a century-fold of home runs," continued Babe Ruth, "will be unobliging pitchers. I mean, the boys on the mound are beginning to know what I pick at for good drives.

"They all know I hate a slow curve. It's no secret. What I like best of all is when they steam over fast ones. Those are the ones I like to nibble on every time.

"Then there's another thing. You know a lot of time a twirler will toss them at me and all around me, but never in line with a good swing. I am not accusing anyone of letting me walk to first intentionally. But you know, I kind of get that feeling."

"How would you explain, shall I say the mechanics, of your home-run swatting?" I asked him.

The big fellow pondered a little while.

"Well, I'll tell you. It's hard to say which element comes first. Coordination, that is perfect timing and harmony of action, is a great essential. You have got to develop rhythm and full utility of every muscle. My whole body goes with every swing. I swing right from the hips. And those who have seen me take a healthy sock at the ball know what I mean. With that coordination there is the fact that I assume that strength is behind it."

During the season, Babe Ruth explained, he weighs around 210. He towers over six feet. His shoulders are broad and massive. Yet there is one incongruity. His wrists are very small.

"So, with this might and brawn which I try to keep in the pink of condition, I cannot help but feel that something is bound to happen to the ball when I lean on it. I might tell you I have another trick of keeping the right foot behind the left, not very

A close-up showing how the Babe gripped the the bat.

The highest-paid pair of batting eyes in the history of baseball carried the Babe to a new world's home-run record last season, breaking his own previous mark.

much. But that helps. I bat left-handed, you know.

"Then the eyes play a great part. Oh, yes, the eyes have got to be well-educated. I would be lost if I didn't have a sense of judgment which the eyes give me.

"As for trying to control the drive itself, I always aim to slam the ball out on a straight line. Pop flies are a little too dangerous. A lusty drive to the bleachers is sure to do the trick.

"There's a little buddy, we must not forget," said Ruth, picking up his bat. "Look it over."

It was very heavy, as bats go. It reminded me of the club of a Neanderthal man.

"It's the heaviest bat in baseball," he said. "It weighs 54 ounces.

"Now that we have the hitting of the ball done away with, there remains another very important job and that is circling the bases. I don't care what anyone says, but a batter is lost, no matter in what part of the field he hits the ball, if he cannot run fast.

"I came to appreciate that fact long ago. I don't do 100 yards in ten flat. But I'd bet I wouldn't come far from it. Being a speedy runner then is another very important factor.

"Of course, when the player is off the diamond, he must not think he can forget his condition. He has got to keep trim all the time. He has to follow a strict code. He must do nothing to impair his physical condition."

Babe Ruth, who has hit 416 home runs in the big leagues since he started with the Boston Red Sox in 1914, has had so glamorous a career that his name means as much to the American boy of today as the names of any three heroes from the pages of history.

"And I'm not through yet by any means, as you can judge what I said about 100 homers," he said. "I am now 33 and expect to be going strong at 44."

Ruth went on to tell the story of his life without any compunction, always clinging to a modest vein.

He was born in Baltimore, Maryland. His father was a factory hand. They were poor. At times his mother had to work in a mill

Knocking out a homer, a series showing Ruth as he steps to bat, facing the pitcher, starting the swing, in mid-swing, and finally, following through after the ball.

to help replenish the family larder.

George Herman Ruth, which is the home-run king's real name, was healthy and husky as a boy. At the age of seven, he was sent to St. Mary's Industrial School in Baltimore. It was there that he got his first inkling of baseball. He started off by being the catcher of the team. In 1913, the school team already had a reputation. Babe Ruth was a southpaw pitcher about whom people were beginning to talk and predict things. He was also a good hitter.

That winter, Jack Dunn, then manager of the Baltimore eastern-league outfit, saw Ruth. The lad was not yet twenty. Dunn wanted Ruth for his team but was told that he could not get him without legally adopting him, because he was still a minor, which he did.

The following season Ruth played with Dunn's team and then was sold to the Boston Americans for $10,000. His salary for that year, 1915, was to be $4,000. The Red Sox conceived the idea of relegating him to the outfield, so that he might conserve his strength when he came to bat.

THROWING HEAT

by JIM KAAT

This article appeared in POPULAR MECHANICS in 2004.

WITH A THREE-RUN
LEAD GOING INTO THE
BOTTOM OF THE
EIGHTH INNING IN
GAME 5 OF THE 2003
AMERICAN LEAGUE
CHAMPIONSHIP
SERIES, NO ONE
WAS THE LEAST BIT
SURPRISED WHEN
NEW YORK YANKEES
MANAGER JOE TORRE
CALLED ON CLOSER
MARIANO RIVERA TO
COME IN AND SHUT
DOWN THE BOSTON
RED SOX.

New York Yankees ace reliever Mariano Rivera is arguably the best closer in the history of baseball.

Rivera, arguably the best closer in the history of baseball, got off to a shaky start, giving up a leadoff triple into the right-field corner by Todd Walker and an RBI groundout by Nomar Garciaparra. The next batter, fearsome slugger Manny Ramirez, had already homered in the game. Another score would bring Boston within one run of the Yankees. It was the classic confrontation—power against power. Ramirez versus Rivera.

But Manny Ramirez had a big advantage. Walking up to the plate, he already knew what Rivera was going to throw him. In fact, all 34,619 fans packed into Fenway Park that night knew what Rivera was going to throw. Essentially, Rivera throws only one pitch—a hard, heavy cut fastball that breaks slightly to the left just as it crosses the plate. Occasionally, he'll also throw a 98-mph four-seam fastball that comes straight across the plate, high in the strike zone. That's it.

Ramirez dug in and peered out at Rivera, gearing up for the fastball. Rivera came set and fired. The four-seamer, 98 miles per hour. Ramirez swung late and missed. Strike one. Rivera had thrown it right by him even though Ramirez knew it was coming. Rivera peered in at catcher Jorge Posada for the sign, came set, and fired. The cutter was low and away at 92 mph. Ramirez, way out in front this time, fouled it off. Strike two. You could see Ramirez scowl at Rivera, a determined look on his face. Ramirez would catch up with the next fastball. And it would be a fastball. He knew that. And he would catch up with it.

Rivera peered in, got the sign, came set, and delivered. A cutter, high and away. Ramirez, fooled, checked his swing and managed to lay off it. Ball one. You could almost hear Ramirez think. The next pitch was going to be a four-seamer. It had to be.

It was.

It was a perfect fastball, textbook perfect. It poured across the plate letter high, 98 mph. Ramirez, simply overmatched even though he had guessed right, swung late and limply. His feeble swing, barely completed as the ball thudded into Posada's mitt, was too little, too late. Rivera, who went on to take Most Valuable Player honors in the ALCS, had proved it again. The fastball is still the best pitch in baseball.

Four-Seamer

Two-Seamer

Dry Spitter

Split-Finger

Not only is the fastball a deadly weapon in its own right, it also is the basis for most pitchers' entire game strategies. Everything works off the fastball. Once you establish your fastball in a game, every batter has to be geared up for it since it might come on any given pitch. Once a pitcher has a batter in this over-tensed, hair-trigger state, it's much easier to fool him with off-speed and breaking pitches.

But it all starts with the fastball.

A fastball may have been the first pitch thrown in a baseball game, the pitcher attempting to simply overpower the batter. Since that first recorded game in 1846, there have been more variations of the fastball developed than any other pitch. Today, you'll find guys throwing a two-seam fastball, a four-seam fastball, a cut fastball, a split-finger fastball, and probably others. Here is a breakdown on how these pitches are thrown.

FOUR-SEAMER: The four-seam fastball is the king of the power pitches and can be delivered with the most accuracy. The grip side view shows how shallow the ball lies in the hand. The ball is held on the wide seams and is thrown over the top. As the ball is released, the fingertips impart straight backspin, with all four seams rotating. This produces a true pitch from the mound to the plate, so there is very little lateral movement.

TWO-SEAMER: The two-seam fastball is gripped with the fingers on the narrow seams. As with the four-seamer, you don't want the ball too deep in the hand; a deeper grip causes more pull and backspin. Fingertip pressure with either the middle or index finger against the seam generates sidespin, which causes the ball to drop as it nears the plate. This late movement is called a sinking or tailing fastball. Hurled by a lefty, the ball will move down and away from a right-handed hitter. Thrown by a right-handed pitcher, the ball will move down and away from a left-handed hitter. Whereas power pitchers favor the four-seam fastball, ground-ball pitchers use the two-seamer more.

THE CUTTER: The cut fastball, or cutter, is thrown using either of the above grips. The key is to keep your hand behind the ball as long as possible and let the grip pressure in the middle finger give it the sidespin or cut. The cutter will move in or out a few inches—like a tight slider—as it nears the plate, but it won't drop like the sinking fastball.

DRY SPITTER (pictured on the opposite page): The dry spitter is thrown with your fingers on the hide as opposed to the seams of the baseball. Before the spitter was made illegal, hurlers would put saliva on the ball to reduce friction, and it would sort of squirt out of their hand like a Ping-Pong ball. These days, the pitcher can have a little coating of mound dirt on his fingers. This also reduces friction. The ball comes out with virtually no spin and will sink as it reaches the plate.

SPLIT-FINGER (pictured on the opposite page): The split-finger fastball is released with relatively little spin. The ball has a tumbling rotation and a late downward movement—similar to the dry spitter. You can change the velocity of the split-finger pitch by varying the position and pressure of your fingers on the ball.

The fastball is the only pitch you can throw to all four quadrants of the strike zone, and it's not used nearly enough today. Look at a pitcher's best games, and I'll bet you'll see a high percentage of fastballs and good control. That's why (ex-Yankee) David Wells was so successful. He favors his fastball, and throws most of them for strikes. His stuff is consistent, from start to start, and he has very few arm problems. He trusts his fastball. To be successful, all pitchers, like Wells, need to trust their fastball and say, here it is, hit it if you can!

THE MYTH OF THE RISING FASTBALL

by PETER BRANCAZIO

Years ago, baseball players and fans commonly believed that it was possible to throw a rising fastball—a pitch that would curve upward or hop as it approached the batter. This could be done, it was thought, by gripping the baseball across the seams and releasing the pitch with a wrist snap that would impart a pronounced backspin on the ball. Although they could not explain why it happened, pitchers, batters, and catchers were convinced that if the pitch was thrown at high speed—more than 90 mph—it would rise as it crossed the plate, causing the batter to misjudge the trajectory and swing under the ball. They were certain the ball rose because they could see it rise.

As a longtime baseball fan and a physicist specializing in the physics of sports, I was curious to find out whether the rising fastball was real. After all, a baseball must obey the laws of physics, and there was a well-established theory and sufficient data available to

>>>

allow me to calculate the aerodynamic forces on a baseball in flight. The basic principles are relatively simple. After the ball leaves the pitcher's hand, it is subject to just three forces: gravity (equal to the weight of the ball) pulling it vertically downward; aerodynamic drag, created by the collision of the ball with the surrounding air, which reduces its forward speed; and what is known as the Magnus force, which is generated by the interaction of the spinning surface of the ball with the air.

The ball generates a low-pressure wake behind it as it moves through the air, but if the surface is spinning, the wake is deflected sideways. According to Newton's law of action and reaction, if the ball deflects the air to one side, the air will push the ball in the opposite direction. The Magnus force always acts perpendicular to the path of the ball, deflecting it sideways according to the direction of spin. It is this force that allows pitchers to throw a repertoire of breaking balls—curveballs, sliders, sinkers, etc.—by adjusting the rate and direction of the spin on the ball along with the speed and location of the pitch. To throw a rising fastball, the Magnus force must be directed upward, opposing the pull of gravity, and this can be achieved by throwing the ball with backspin. If the Magnus force is greater than the weight of the ball, then the net force on the ball will cause it to rise.

When I ran computer simulations of pitches, I made some interesting discoveries. I learned that over the standard pitching distance of 60 feet 6 inches, a ball loses about 9 percent of its initial speed due to aerodynamic drag—thus, a pitch launched at 90 mph will have slowed to 81 mph when it reaches the batter. The pitch takes only about 0.44 seconds to cover the distance. During this interval the ball falls about three feet due to the pull of gravity. A batter has less than half a second to judge the trajectory of the ball, decide whether to swing, and then bring his bat around to the projected point of contact.

Hitting a baseball at the major-league level, I discovered, is a truly remarkable feat. Most significantly, I discovered that in order for the ball to truly rise in flight—for the Magnus force to exceed the weight of the ball—the pitch would have to be launched with a backspin of more than 3,600 rpm. This is far beyond the capacity of any major-league pitcher. High-speed photography shows that spin rates of about 1,800 rpm are the best that can be achieved. Thus, it is not humanly possible to throw a true rising fastball. With the ball spinning at 1,800 rpm and traveling at 90 mph, the Magnus force retards the vertical drop by a little more than a foot.

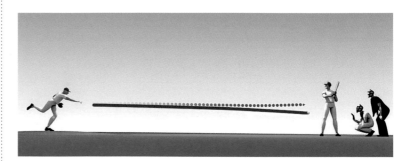

Pitchers, batters, and catchers swear that a ball can rise at the plate.

Instead of dropping three feet vertically on its way to the plate, the ball drops slightly less than two feet. I concluded that the rising fastball is an optical illusion. The ball appears to rise only because it doesn't fall as much as the batter expects it to—in other words, the ball rises only in relation to the batter's expectations. To the exquisitely trained eyes of a top-flight batter or catcher, the ball appears to rise because it does not fall as much as it would without the backspin.

Over time, a number of other scientists have verified my results. The most convincing confirmation has come from real-time tracking of baseball pitches using multiple video cameras and rapid computerized reconstruction of the trajectories. To the best of my knowledge, no one has ever recorded a fastball rising as it crosses the plate.

THE CATCHER TRADES IN A MASK FOR A HELMET

Why do baseball catchers now look like goalies on a hockey team? Blame it on Canada. Charlie O'Brien, at that time a star catcher for the Toronto Blue Jays, was watching a hockey game and was struck how goalies simply shrugged off puck hits to their helmet. After working with Van Velden Mask Inc. and Major League Baseball, O'Brien developed a catcher's helmet called the All-Star MVP that was approved by Major League Baseball in 1996 and has since caught on everywhere.

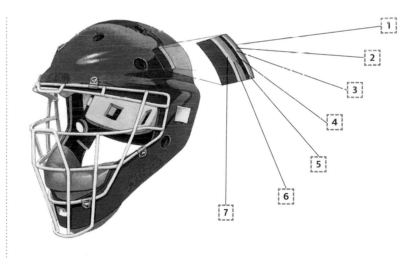

The All-Star MVP helmet is composed of seven layers. From the outside in:

1. Gelcoat   **2.** 102-strand fiberglass   **3.** Woven roving   **4.** Kevlar
5. Kevlar   **6.** 102-strand fiberglass   **7.** Fine-mesh boat cloth

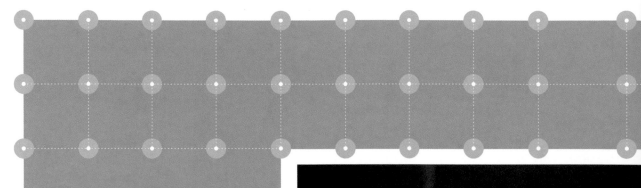

THE BREAKING PITCH

by JIM KAAT

This article was published in
POPULAR MECHANICS in 1997.

IT IS GAME 3 OF THE 1996 WORLD SERIES. THE ATLANTA BRAVES HAVE ALREADY TAKEN THE FIRST TWO GAMES IN THE BRONX. IF THEY CAN BEAT THE YANKEES IN ATLANTA'S FULTON COUNTY STADIUM, THEY'LL HOLD A SEEMINGLY INSURMOUNTABLE 3–0 LEAD IN THE SERIES, AND THE YANKEES CAN HANG IT UP UNTIL NEXT YEAR.

As a major-league pitcher for 25 years, left-hander Jim Kaat won 283 games and earned sixteen Gold Glove Awards.

But things have gone the Yankees' way in this game. A courageous effort by starting pitcher David Cone and excellent support by relievers Mariano Rivera and Graeme Lloyd have kept the Braves' big bats in check, and going into the bottom of the ninth, it is 5–2 Yankees as ace reliever John Wetteland takes the mound.

Wetteland is known for his blazing 99-mph fastball, and there is no reason for first batter Javier Lopez to look for anything else. Sure enough, Wetteland feeds Lopez nothing but heat, and all Lopez can do is ground feebly to Derek Jeter at short. But in his haste to make the play, Jeter bobbles the ball and Lopez is on.

Andruw Jones comes up. Jones, a rookie, has fed on Yankee pitching the first two games of the Series, including a couple of homers. A home run here and Atlanta is within one.

Wetteland bears down and brings heat. Jones looks at fastball after fastball, managing to foul a couple off and take a couple of balls. With the count two and two, Jones gears up for yet another fastball as Wetteland comes set and checks the runner. At almost 100 mph, Wetteland's fastball reaches home plate in less than half a second. Jones will have to start his swing before Wetteland actually releases the ball if he is to have any hope whatsoever of hitting it.

Wetteland deals. Jones starts his bat and begins to stride. The ball is released. But wait. Jones recognizes the spin on the ball. He sees the stitches. Oh, no! It isn't a fastball. It's a breaking ball. Jones tries to hold back his swing. His front leg has started to move. He holds back mightily. His left knee visibly buckles, but he holds back. He can't pull the trigger. His only hope is that the pitch will be called a ball.

"Steeeeh!" screams plate umpire Tim Welke.

Strike three.

Such is the power of the unexpected breaking pitch in baseball, especially when a power pitcher like John Wetteland sets it up with one fastball after another. In fact, in this game the next batter, Jeff Blauser, strikes out on three straight fastballs and pinch hitter Terry Pendleton grounds weakly to second to end the game. Knowing that Wetteland can throw a breaking ball at any moment is a weapon in itself. It throws off the batter's timing and prevents a hitter from merely sitting on a pitcher's fastball.

The breaking pitch—curveball, split-finger, slurve, slider, and other variations—has been around since baseball began. But never have so many pitchers thrown so many different breaking pitches with so many different looks as today. Pity the poor batter who has to decide what he is going to do with any given pitch in less than the one second it takes for the ball to leave the pitcher's hand and reach the hitting zone.

At one time, a batter could look for a fastball but was able to adjust to a breaking pitch that started out wide of the strike zone and then broke over the plate, or a breaking pitch that started high off the strike zone and broke down into it. Today, most breaking pitches move only an inch or two within the strike zone. And that's all it takes to cause a batter to miss or to hit the ball feebly. And today, breaking pitches move left, right, down, diagonally, and with variations on all of the above.

For years, the questions were whether a breaking pitch actually curved or whether it was just an optical illusion, or even simply a matter of trajectory. But now, with the availability of laser-based, computerized optical systems, it has been proven that the ball actually changes its flight path on the way to home plate.

As a former major-league pitcher, I threw thousands of breaking balls in my career. Frankly, I don't know why any of them curved as they left my hand. What I can tell you is that I can make a ball curve, slide, break, or drop. Much of the movement of the ball is controlled by the way it is gripped and released.

MECHANICS OF THE BREAKING PITCH

Breaking pitches spin, which results from applying finger pressure to the ball and snapping your wrist when releasing it. You'll get maximum spin by gripping the ball deeply within the fingers so that they wrap entirely around the ball, but your thumb has to be relaxed. I had an exercise I did when I was coaching pitchers. I'd say, "Squeeze the ball as tight as you can with your thumb and move your wrist." It didn't move very easily. But if you curl your fingers around the ball and barely lay your thumb on it, your entire wrist loosens up so you can snap it to get maximum spin.

The other element in a fast breaking pitch, such as the slider, is velocity. The key here is to stay behind the ball until the last possible second. Then, apply the wrist action for the particular pitch you're throwing. If you start rotating your wrist too early in the pitch, you lose velocity and get a slower, sloppier spin.

Sinking fastball:
Sidespin and backspin are generated by finger-tip pressure with either the index or middle finger on the seam when the ball is released.

Curveball: The palm is turned inward with a release as if you're pulling down on the ball. Sidespin and backspin should be imparted with the wrist, not the elbow.

Screwball: The palm is turned out on the release, and the ball breaks to the outside against right-handed hitters. Velocity is slower than that of a curveball.

While no two hurlers have exactly the same style of pitching, all of them strive for a consistent delivery in terms of arm angle and release point. The batter draws an imaginary rectangular box right where the pitcher releases the ball, and he looks for clues in that area as to what type of pitch will be coming at him. If the pitcher drops his arm a bit when he delivers a curveball, for instance, the batter will pick up on this and know when to expect a curve. Snapping the wrist on the release should happen so quickly that the batter can't pick up on it early in the delivery. Good hitters say they can recognize the curveball when it gets a particular distance from home plate. It happens so fast that they can't really see it until the ball gets close to home plate. They used to say Ted Williams could pick up a pitch right out of the hand. I don't think anyone can pick it up that quickly.

SINKING FASTBALL

(Pictured on the opposite page.) Looking at specific breaking pitches, the two-seam fastball, also called a moving or sinking fastball, is gripped on the top of the ball with the narrow seams exposed. This is in contrast to the four-seam fastball, which must be gripped on the wide seams to get it to travel in a true trajectory with all seams rotating. Both of these pitches are released with backspin.

When releasing this fastball, you usually apply pressure against the seam with either the index or middle finger. It's a matter of preference. This imparts the sidespin that causes the ball to drop.

CURVEBALL

Years ago, this pitch was called a drop. I throw a curve with a twelve o'clock to six o'clock rotation. This release imparts sidespin and backspin because I maintain pressure on the ball with my middle finger while rolling it over the top of my index finger. I like to throw the ball into the wind because this increases the ball's rotation and helps the break. The key to the curveball is to keep your hand behind the ball as long as possible, impart the spin with the wrist and not with the elbow, and make sure the thumb is relaxed. I shorten my stride by one inch or so, compared to pitching a fastball. The object here is not to be throwing the ball toward the batter. You want a feeling as if you're pulling down on the ball, almost as if you're throwing it into the ground. This type of motion gives the ball the desired trajectory.

SCREWBALL

The screwball is actually the opposite of the curveball in terms of snapping the wrist. Whereas I grip and release the ball with my

Forkball: Also called the splitter, the ball is released with a lot of velocity but with a tumbling rotation for a dramatic drop at the plate.

Slider: Releasing the ball off the index finger also imparts backspin and sidespin, causing lateral and downward movement.

palm turned inward for the curve, I turn my palm out when I'm throwing a screwball—almost as if I'm turning a screwdriver.

The ball's trajectory is similar to a curve, but it can't be thrown quite as hard. So the velocity is less than that of a curveball. Also, the ball breaks outward instead of inward. Left-handed pitchers like to throw screwballs to right-handed hitters because the ball starts toward the middle of the plate and then breaks away to the outside corner.

FORKBALL

The forkball, also known as the splitter, is an interesting pitch. You jam the ball between your first two fingers as hard as you can and you deliver it with the same action as a fastball, with the wrist coming straight over from the 12 to 6 o'clock position. The ball travels with a lot of velocity but with a tumbling kind of rotation. The rotation slows down as the ball approaches the plate, and if delivered correctly, the bottom kind of falls out of it.

SLIDER

The hard slider or short curve, as I used to call it, has a certain amount of lateral break and a certain amount of down break. It's a faster pitch than a curve, but it's slower than a fastball, and it has a shorter break than a curveball. If you judged the pitch by mph, and a pitcher's fastball is, say, 90 mph, and his curveball is 80 mph, he would want the slider to be in the 86-to-87-mph range. The harder you throw a slider, the shorter and quicker break you can get on it. The release technique is between a curve and a fastball.

Some pitchers release the ball off their middle finger. I throw my slider off my index finger. I try to feel as if I'm wiping over the outside of the ball as I snap on it in order to give it some backspin and sidespin.

OTHER VARIATIONS

A lot of pitchers today throw a slurve. They pitch the slider as if they are throwing a curve, and the ball comes out in a big, sweeping flat curve. I consider this pitch to be just a rather sloppy slider. It has a much wider break than the slider was intended to have, and I think this is one of the reasons there are so many more home runs today than years ago. Pitchers like Tom Seaver of the New York Mets could throw a true slider, whereas pitchers today would call that a cut fastball. A true slider breaks late and moves three or four inches—sort of a little slide. A true slider should be more of a power pitch. Pitchers today use the slider more as a breaking ball or an off-speed pitch.

Of all my pitches, the one that brings up the fondest memory is the slider. I remember a game in the late 1960s when I threw a really hard slider down and away to strike out Red Sox slugger Carl Yastrzemski to end the game with men on. Striking out Carl was pretty hard to do. I remember seeing that ball break. I threw a similar pitch to Don Zimmer in 1965, when I was playing for the Minnesota Twins, for the last out against the Washington Senators to clinch the pennant. When the ball comes out of your hand, you can almost feel whether it's going to have a good break or a little slip to it. Both of those balls felt really crisp coming out, and they both broke in the same spot. I still remember that distinctly. I wonder if Yastrzemski and Zim do?

THE PHYSICS OF A CURVEBALL
by PETER BRANCAZIO

For years, many scientists believed that the curveball was an optical illusion. As we shall see, this is not true. In fact, physicists have long been aware of the fact that a spinning ball curves in flight, going back to Sir Isaac Newton, who wrote a paper on the subject in 1671.

In 1852, the German physicist Gustav Magnus revived the topic when he demonstrated in an experiment that when a spinning object moves through a fluid, it experiences a sideways force. This phenomenon, now known as the Magnus effect, is the fundamental principle behind the curved flight of any spinning ball.

THE MAGNUS EFFECT
The theory of the Magnus effect is a relatively simple exercise in aerodynamics. When any object is moving through the air, its surface interacts with a thin layer of air known as the boundary layer. In the case of a sphere, which has a very poor aerodynamic shape, the air in the boundary layers peels away from the surface, creating a "wake"

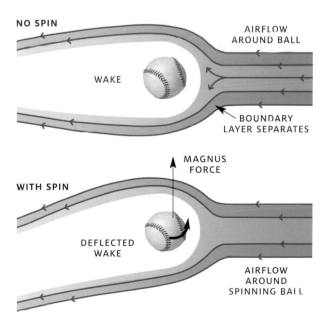

NO SPIN

AIRFLOW AROUND BALL

WAKE

BOUNDARY LAYER SEPARATES

MAGNUS FORCE

WITH SPIN

DEFLECTED WAKE

AIRFLOW AROUND SPINNING BALL

>>>

or lower-pressure region behind the ball. The front-to-back pressure difference creates a backward force on the ball, which slows its forward motion. This is the normal air resistance, or aerodynamic drag, that acts on any object moving through the air. However, if the sphere is spinning as it moves, the boundary layer separates at different points on opposite sides of the ball—further upstream on the side of the ball that is turning into the airflow, and further downstream on the side of the ball turning backward. As a consequence, the air flowing around the ball is deflected slightly sideways, resulting in an asymmetrical wake behind the ball. The effect is to generate a pressure difference across the ball, creating a lateral force component that pushes the ball sideways. This lateral force, at right angles to the forward motion of the ball, is known as the Magnus force.

THE MAGNUS FORCE

The strength of the Magnus force is in direct proportion to the rate of spin as well as the forward speed of the ball—the greater the forward speed, the greater the force. It will also be proportional to the air

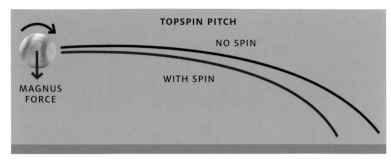

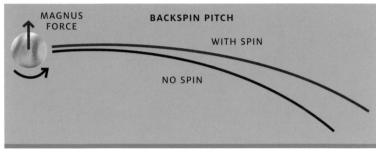

density, which means that a ball will tend to curve less at higher altitudes where the air is thinner—a boon to hitters in a high-altitude city like Denver. The stitches on the baseball also help increase the Magnus force—not only by increasing the thickness of the boundary layer, but also by providing a place for the pitcher to put his fingers so he can put more spin on the ball. It should be noted, however, that stitches are not required to make a ball curve. Even a smooth-surfaced table tennis ball will curve if it is given enough spin.

On the other hand, the direction of the Magnus

force depends only on the direction of spin. As shown in the diagram above, the force is always directed toward the side of the ball that is turning backward. In other words, the Magnus force always points in the same direction that the front of the ball is turning.

DIRECTING THE BALL

By properly orienting the spin direction, a pitcher can make the Magnus force point in any direction—left, right, up, down, and so on. For example, the natural clockwise rotation of a right-hander's wrist creates a leftward force (from the pitcher's perspective) that causes the ball to curve away from a right-handed batter. When thrown with three-quarters overhand motion, the same pitch will curve down and away from the batter. Conversely, a left-handed pitcher's natural wrist rotation (which is counterclockwise) causes the ball to curve left to right—that is, into a right-handed batter and away from a left-hander. In order for a right-handed pitcher to imitate this motion of throwing the pitch known as the screwball, he must turn his wrist counterclockwise as he releases the ball—an unnatural, uncomfortable motion that frequently leads to elbow trouble. Much of the strategy of baseball is a direct consequence of the fact that right-handers and left-handers throw different pitches, simply because of a quirk of human physiology that makes our hands rotate more easily in one direction than the other.

A ball can be made to curve in a vertical plane as well. In fact, the trajectory of any thrown pitch has a natural downward curvature due to the force of gravity. However, by changing the spin direction, a pitcher can increase or decrease the curvature. For example, when a ball is thrown with topspin, the Magnus force will act toward the ground,

causing it to curve more sharply. If the ball is thrown with backspin, the Magnus force will point away from the ground, causing the ball to curve less. The latter pitch produces what is often called a rising fastball. However, the laws of aerodynamics tell us that for a baseball to physically rise, (that is, curve upward) as it approaches the batter, the Magnus force would have to be greater than the weight of the ball—an impossible feat for any human. For a full explanation of science behind this pitch, see "The Myth of the Rising Fastball" on page 55.

It seems pretty clear that no right-minded physicist would ever argue that a curveball is an illusion. However, as with the case of the rising fastball, we will argue that the sharp break of a curveball is illusory. While many hitters often report that a good overhand curveball breaks so sharply that it looks as if it is falling off a table, the laws of aerodynamics clearly show that the Magnus force cannot suddenly increase in flight—as would be required for a sudden change in curvature—but can only get smaller as the spin and speed of the ball slow down. The explanation for this illusion has to do with how

the batter perceives the flight of the ball. The angular motion of the ball—that is, its apparent motion across a batter's field of vision—seems relatively slow at first, but then increases as the ball approaches. In fact, it has been demonstrated that the angular motion becomes so rapid that no batter could possibly move his head fast enough to keep his eye on the ball all the way. When a good curveball is thrown, the change in its angular motion becomes even more pronounced as it nears the batter, greatly enhancing the appearance of its natural curvature and giving the illusion of a sharp bend.

MYSTERY PITCH

by DAVIN COBURN

It's quickly becoming the Bigfoot of baseball, an urban legend born in a Japanese lab and racing across the Internet. They call it the gyroball—the exact translation is probably closer to Demon Sphere Gyro Ball—and it's either the first new pitch in nearly four decades or a complete and total sham.

Five years ago, computer scientist Ryutaro Himeno was testing super-computers by modeling the fluid dynamics of airflow around baseballs. Himeno's deconstruction of existing pitches led to a strange new one—whirling clockwise as it flew forward, the virtual ball curved as abruptly as its closest relative, the slider,

but without sinking. Himeno met with Kazushi Tezuka, who runs baseball training centers in Tokyo and Osaka, and they ironed out the pitch's mechanics.

As detailed in the books the pair has since authored, a gyroball calls for a complex flip of the fingers during release, ending with the thumb pointed down. At its most effective, the pitch breaks horizontally

>>>

In theory, the gyroball uses a twisting release to put counterclockwise spin on the ball (from the batter's view), making it break much flatter than other pitches.

as it nears the batter, as though shrugging off gravity.

It's one thing to hypothesize a new pitch. It's another to throw one. Japanese pitching phenomenon Daisuke Matsuzaka, who led Japan to the World Baseball Classic championship in March 2007, says he's thrown gyroballs. "I have done it in a game," Matsuzaka told Yahoo!

Daisuke Matsuzaka, Boston Red Sox pitcher and World Baseball Classic MVP, claims he can throw gyroballs.

Sports. "But not too much. Sometimes accidentally." Gyroball theorists point to slo-mo video of Matsuzaka in action and photos taken of his thumb-down follow-through as further evidence.

Himeno, director of the Advanced Center for Computing and Communication in Japan, says that by 2006 Matsuzaka was not the only one throwing the pitch. "I do not know much about pitchers playing in either Japan or the United States but at least Mr. Matsuzaka (now of the Boston Red Sox) and Shunsuke Watanabe (of the Chiba Lotte Marines) pitch the gyroball," says Himeno.

But all of the so-called evidence is subjective. One pitching coach showed POPULAR MECHANICS a video of an Indiana high schooler named Joey Niezer supposedly throwing a gyroball, at the urging of Will Carrol, a writer for *Baseball Prospectus*. "They said throw it like a football—to bring it back past my ear and push down with my fingers when I release it," said Niezer, who used the pitch sparingly. Niezer's pitching coach at Oldenburg Academy, William Burke, says the pitch "breaks really hard

and virtually flat. People talk about a 12–6 curver; this would be 9–3. And it can be thrown with relative ease, compared to snapping off a hard slider."

Niezer has since stopped throwing the gyroball, and Niezer's college coach at Wabash, Cory Stevens, remains unconvinced after watching video replays of the gyroball in action. "Joey's pitch in that video looks like a curve," says Steven. "And that Japanese video [of Matsuzaka] looks like a slider to me."

Himeno has another take. "Some sorts of sliders or cut fastballs are considered one variation of the gyroball," he says. "In that sense, many pitchers are actually pitching it."

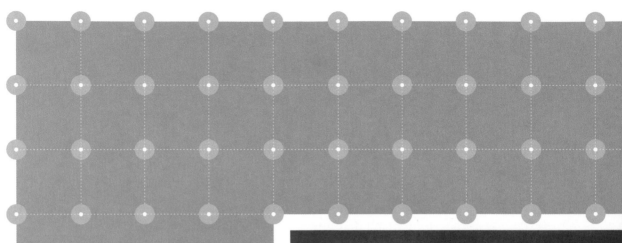

PITCHING 1949

by AUBREY O. COOKMAN JR.

Baseball comes cloaked in a mantle of history unlike any other sport. Names like Mantle, Mays, Koufax, and many others are the stuff of legend. As this article published in 1949 (originally titled "Taking A Lesson from Champion Pitchers") demonstrates, the names of the players may have changed, but the skills used by pitchers of the 1940s (Carl Hubbell, Early Wynn, and Bob Feller, to name just three) are as familiar now as they were then.

WHAT DOES IT TAKE TO BE A BIG-LEAGUE PITCHER? EXPERTS IN THE BEST POSITION TO OBSERVE, LIKE CATCHER JIM HEGAN OF THE WORLD CHAMPION CLEVELAND INDIANS, GENERALLY AGREE THAT SPEED AND CONTROL ARE THE BIGGEST FACTORS. THE GAME'S GREAT PITCHERS HAVE VARIED WIDELY IN SIZE, SHAPE, AND TEMPERAMENT, AND MANY WERE FAMOUS FOR A PARTICULAR KIND OF PITCH, BUT EVERY ONE HAD BETTER-THAN-AVERAGE SPEED AND FINE CONTROL.

Bob Lemon struck out 1,277 batters for the Cleveland Indians during the course of his career (1946–58).

MASTERING CONTROL

Hegan knows how star hurlers perform. He catches a Cleveland staff that has been called the best ever assembled on one team. Two of its members, Bob Lemon and Gene Bearden, were twenty-game winners last season. A third, Bobby Feller, with nearly 200 major-league victories and over 2,000 strikeouts to his credit, ranks as one of baseball's all-time greats. A government-timing device clocked Feller's fast one at 99.5 mph. Batters have a split second to decide whether or not to swing with the ball hurtling toward them from only 60 feet 6 inches away—the distance between the mound and home plate. But even with his natural speed, Feller couldn't climb to stardom until he mastered control.

Some pitchers laid the groundwork for good control as youngsters by throwing for hours at a time at stationary targets. Some would pitch stones or balls at a hole in the fence. Others have rigged up "picture frames" of canvas or poles, with a 17-inch wide and 38- or 39-inch-high opening representing the strike zone for an average-size batter.

Reduced to its simplest explanation, pitching skill is the ability to throw consistently what the batter least expects or wants. Watching the pitchers work from Hegan's vantage point behind the plate, you get a better idea of the finesse that makes a champion.

GIVING AWAY THE PITCH

Deceiving sharp-eyed big leaguers takes grade-A performance at all times. In their constant duel of wits, the pitcher can't afford to give the batter any inkling as to what kind of a pitch he'll serve up. Coaches and rival players are watching him constantly for telltale signs. Unconscious mannerisms sometimes betray a rookie pitcher's intentions. George Earnshaw of the Philadelphia Athletics originally had a habit of scuffing the ground around the mound with his toe when catchers flashed the curve sign, while the call for a fastball brought no such response. Until corrected, it was like posting an announcement each time for the hitter.

Urban "Red" Faber of the Chicago White Sox, a famous spitball pitcher, would overdo preparations for the saliva-applying

Dizzy Dean is best remembered as leader of the St. Louis Cardinals' "Gas House Gang" in 1934 as he posted a record of 30 wins and seven losses.

operations when he was faking his favorite delivery. Opponents noting the exaggerated facial contortions could be reasonably sure Faber's wicked "spitter" wasn't shortly coming their way. Babe Ruth, in his youthful pitching days, would unconsciously stick out his tongue when preparing to throw a curve. Others have unknowingly tipped off rivals by hitching up their shoulders prior to a certain type pitch, or crooking their wrist significantly during the start of the windup.

Managers and coaches are always on the alert to detect and correct these faults in their players. Occasionally a cagey pitcher will use these "giveaways" to his advantage in double-crossing rivals. Dizzy Dean (St. Louis Cardinals, Chicago Cubs, and St. Louis Browns, 1930–47) used to allow the opposition to "discover" his preliminaries for a certain type pitch, adding to its authenticity by using it a few times in the expected manner, then crossing them up at crucial moments by switching at the last minute to a completely different kind of pitch.

Coaches teach youngsters to deliver all pitches with the same motion, generally a three-quarter style, about midway between sidearm and overhand. Except for a few freak specialty pitches, the fingering—the way the ball is gripped—is basically the same for all pitches. A smart pitcher masks the fingering with his gloved hand. For about 75 percent of all pitches, the forefinger and second finger are on top of the ball, the thumb is below it, and the two remaining fingers fold down against the palm. Most experts advocate gripping the ball across the seams, rather than with them, to get better control.

TYPES OF PITCHES

A fastball behaves differently from a curve because of the way the ball is released. There isn't time then for a batter to react to the knowledge, even if he had it. Fastballs leave the hand with a downward snap of the wrist. A good, "live" pitch, in baseball parlance, seems to shoot upward when it nears the batter. One that comes straight and level across the plate is easy to hit, despite its speed, and it travels farther than breaking-type pitches.

Though held the same, a curve is thrown with an outward snap of the wrist so that the back of the pitcher's hand ends up facing the plate. The ball rolls off the first two fingers. Most effective curveballers put pressure on the second finger, just before the release, and use the first solely as a guide. The ball has to be made to spin in order to curve.

Some hurlers finger a slow ball, or "change up," just as they do a fastball or curve, but lift the top two fingers just as the ball is

Carl Hubbell led the New York Giants to three pennants in five years during the 1930s with a devastating screwball.

Bob Feller (1936–56) of the Cleveland Indians led the American League in strikeouts for seven years. For his career, Feller struck out 2,581 batters.

released. When thrown with the same motion as a fast one—except for the last-second wrist snap—it throws a batter's timing off badly.

The sharpest change of pace in baseball today is the "blooper ball" thrown by Rip Sewell of Pittsburgh. It floats plateward so slowly that batters can see the ball's seams and it arches down to them from as high as twelve to fifteen feet, but Rip uses it sparingly, and hitters aren't able to adjust their timing for solid swings.

Among the most effective "extra" deliveries is the knuckler. Manager Lou Boudreau of Cleveland claims it is the most baffling ball his star Bearden throws. Bearden grips it with the nails of his first three fingers and the sphere sails up to the plate with virtually no spin, breaking downward. Some knucklers, like Dutch Leonard of the Chicago Cubs, hold it with two fingers on top, pressing the first joints against the ball.

Carl Hubbell, the former New York Giant southpaw, perfected a screwball that he held just like a curve. The difference was in the inward snap he gave the ball on release, ending up with his palm facing the batter. This spin made the ball act like a reverse curve.

Early Wynn, another Cleveland star, has a bothersome slider that he grips like a curve, but holds slightly off center, and throws with less wrist snap. It breaks several inches but, unlike the curve, it "slides" away from right-handed batters without breaking downward.

USING YOUR RESOURCES

Some of the more methodical hurlers keep notebooks in which they jot down the data on the batting strengths and weaknesses of rivals. When a hitter like Rudy York (277 home runs over a thirteen-year career with the Detroit Tigers, Boston Red Sox, Chicago White Sox, and Philadelphia Athletics, 1934–48) displays a liking for pitches that catch the outside edge of the plate, it is pretty certain he'll never get one there when the game is close. Hurlers have equally long memories for weak points. Feller, who has been playing against Joe DiMaggio for ten years, thinks the Yankee star normally does the least damage to a ball that breaks low, on the outside corner.

Catchers are important to pitchers in analyzing the batter's stance and swing. This is particularly true when a newcomer is at bat. If he is a plate-crowder, the catcher will probably call for balls that break in close to his bat handle. Or, if he stands too far back, the catcher might ask for a curve or a fastball that nicks the corner.

FOUL BALL! TRICKY PITCHES, FREAKY BATS

by JIM KAAT

This article was published in POPULAR MECHANICS in 1988.

FOR ALL THE WRONG REASONS, 1987 WAS ONE OF THE MORE MEMORABLE SEASONS IN BASEBALL. THREE PLAYERS WERE PENALIZED FOR A DUBIOUS SORT OF ACHIEVEMENT. THESE PLAYERS WERE PENALIZED UNDER THE RULES THAT PROHIBIT THE DEFACING OF BALLS OR THE USE OF FREAK BATS. THAT RULE—AGAINST PITCHING A BALL THAT HAS BEEN ROUGHENED, WET, POLISHED, OR OTHERWISE TAMPERED WITH—ENTERED THE BOOKS IN 1920.

The Chicago Cubs' Sammy Sosa breaks his bat on a first-inning ground ball at Wrigley Field in Chicago on June 3, 2003. After the play, home-plate umpire Tim McClelland examined the bat and ejected Sosa after finding cork in the bat. Sosa said he mistakenly used a bat otherwise used only in batting practice.

Through 1980, a period of 60 years, only two pitchers had ever been disciplined. That number was matched in 1987 when Joe Niekro of the Minnesota Twins and Kevin Gross of the Philadelphia Phillies each received a ten-day suspension for bringing to the mound an abrasive that might be used to scuff the ball—sandpaper in the case of Gross, an emery board in the case of Niekro. And when the bat shattered in the hands of Houston's Billy Hatcher on the night of September 1 and was found to contain cork, Hatcher got an involuntary vacation with pay and his manager got to pay a fine.

There's no doubt that the subjects of illegal pitches and doctored bats received more attention in 1987 than any season before, despite the fact that they had to share the limelight with questions about the allegedly livelier ball.

From my perspective in the broadcast booth, from talking to players off-camera, and from my own experience in the game, I believe that the percentage of pitchers and batters who break the rules on a consistent basis is actually very small. At the same time, I believe that because of certain changes in the game over the past twenty years or so, there is probably a greater tendency and temptation today to look for an edge, whether it is a legal one, like the split-fingered fastball, or trying to simulate the splitter's movement by loading the ball.

THE BATTER'S ADVANTAGE

It's a fact that batters are muscling up, swinging lighter bats, and swinging them more aggressively. And why not? The effective strike zone is smaller than ever before, so a pitcher really has a tougher time keeping the ball off the fat of the bat.

What the pitchers are throwing, from amateur ball to the majors, is more off-speed stuff and breaking balls, including the split-fingered fastball. Fewer pitchers are challenging the batter with natural, live, trust-your-stuff fastballs, especially during the late innings of a close game. Have you noticed the inordinate number of late-inning, often game-winning home runs hit off a breaking ball? That kind of pitch loses its crispness when the thrower gets arm-weary, and it tends to hang. The same goes for

When umps nabbed Twins pitcher Joe Niekro with an emery board in the summer of 1987, he was suspended for leaving a different mark on the ball.

split-fingered fastballs, scuffballs, and even sliders, although these take their toll in swinging third strikes too, especially with more batters swinging wildly instead of merely trying to make contact.

Speaking of the fences, they keep getting closer and closer in today's ballparks. Besides these factors, higher temperatures and humidity can turn a few fly balls into home runs. Dr. Robert Watts, a mechanical engineer at Tulane University, actually computed how far a ball will travel on a hot, humid day compared to a cool, dry one. Watts says that a ball might carry twenty feet farther under warm, moist conditions, where the air density actually decreases, thereby exerting less drag.

A DIFFERENT BALL?

All the talk about trick pitches, corked bats, livelier balls, and whatnot in 1987 sparked a good deal of research and speculation in many science labs all around the country. The belief was widespread among baseball professionals that the ball was livelier in 1987 than in 1986. I believe so myself, from the miracles I've seen flying out of places that are not hitters' ballparks.

Nonetheless, the leagues conducted lab tests around mid-season and announced that the ball's coefficient of restitution—a measurement of how well (or how poorly) the ball bounces back upon hitting a hard surface—was no different than in 1986. After being fired by machine and colliding at an initial velocity of 85 feet per second—58 mph—a major-league baseball must show a coefficient of restitution between 51.4 and 57.8 percent. If it's any higher, the ball is too lively. If it's any lower, it's something only a pitcher could love. The size and weight of the balls were also within the tolerances permitted.

If the 1987 ball didn't have more hop, then another ball-related factor might account for why so many missiles went into orbit. Dr. Joel Hollenberg, of the prestigious Cooper Union engineering school in New York, speculates that the stitches might impart some extra mileage. Since the early 1980s, Hollenberg has studied the aerodynamic forces that cause the knuckleball to behave in its erratic fashion. His research shows that the knuckler's shifting sideways motion is determined by the orientation of the ball's stitches against the airflow as the pitch travels to the plate.

In 1987, Hollenberg reran some of his 1983 experiments, but with 1987 major-league balls. His data on drag kept coming out differently. The only variable, he realized, could be a different texture to the stitches. After repeated tests the evidence just stared him in the face: he describes the stitching as rougher, or more pronounced. Others have noticed the 1987 ball's stitching seemed slightly more raised than usual. That type of ball is usually a pitcher's delight.

Besides the number of stitches and type of string, the major-league specifications aren't too specific about stitching. If they are higher, this means the shape of the ball is rougher—uniformly round but nor uniformly smooth. You might be surprised to learn that Hollenberg and others state that a rough sphere is more aerodynamic than a smooth one. This is the secret behind the golf ball, with its 336 dimples. It seems that the roughness creates a more turbulent airflow around the ball, which has the effect of breaking up or reducing the ball's wake. The invisible wake exerts drag on the ball. But if the wake is reduced, the ball travels farther.

A somewhat related hypothesis, from Dr. Peter Brancazio of Brooklyn College's physics department, contends that a scuff on the ball might play a similar role in reducing drag. Brancazio and others point out that this would depend upon the ball's rate of spin, the degree of scuffing, and the position of the scuff in relation to the ball's direction of spin.

You'll rarely find a scofflaw who admits to it while he's an active player, as did Gaylord Perry and Bill "Spaceman" Lee. But the list of felons who've confessed after retirement includes Whitey Ford, Jim Brosnan, George Bamberger, and the angelic-sounding duo of Schoolboy Rowe and Preacher Roe. Even Bill Kunkel, the American League umpire and former pitcher, once indicated he could detect a spitball from hands-on experience.

SPITBALLS

To make what is commonly called a spitball effective, the pitcher must make the surface of the ball as smooth as possible in the area where he will grip it, which is on the covers, never the seams. The object is to eliminate friction in the grip so that the ball has no rotation or spin when it's released.

Preparing the smooth surface can be accomplished by the wet or dry method. The ball can be moistened with saliva, which can become a little slicker when the ball-doctor chews lozenges made from the bark of the slippery elm tree. More up-to-date pharmaceuticals include lubricants such as K-Y Jelly and petroleum jelly. Soap will do the trick too. Usually, these substances are smeared on the pitcher's skin, hair, or uniform, and they're difficult for an umpire to detect.

The dry spitter can be prepared with powdery materials. Talcum will work. And I clearly recall that the mound in Cleveland has fine, filmy dirt that's perfect for the task. Getting some on your finger is literally as easy as tying your shoes.

Wet-head or dry-look, the spitter is thrown with the same motion and velocity as the fastball. But when it's released—and it virtually squirts out between the fingers, as a Ping-Pong ball would if you pinched it—it has none of the fast rotation that a pitcher would usually want on a pitch. As a result, the ball meets air resistance and suddenly, very suddenly, loses velocity and drops straight down.

SCUFFBALLS

With scuffballs and cut balls the break is sideways, left or right. Either way, the break comes late—after the batter has judged where the ball will be. Here, you want to generate friction with the ball, and that's what abrasion achieves.

The pitch is thrown with a fastball grip, fastball delivery, and usually at fastball speed. The way a pitcher grips his fastball determines where the ball gets scuffed. But to break sideways, the scuff must remain the same spot, perpendicular to the direction of the pitch as the ball spins bottom over top toward the plate.

Because the ball is rougher on one side, that spot creates turbulence in that air that flows over it on the way home. As Watts and others explain, the turbulent air peels away from the rough spot, making the air's wake shift around the smoother side of the ball. This causes an imbalance that redirects the airflow and forces the ball to veer to the scuffed side.

If science has demystified what the scuff does to the ball, how it gets on the ball remains a total mystery to any pitcher who has ever been confronted by an umpire.

Of course, baseballs do get nicked and scratched in the normal course of duty. A foul off the backstop or a sharp grounder, especially on artificial turf, will leave scars. That's found money. The man-made variety takes more ingenuity.

In the days when most uniforms had belts, some pitchers might sharpen the buckle so they could cut shallow grooves in the ball while contemplating signs from the catcher. Double knits banished the buckle, but resourceful pitchers might conceal a needle, tack, or other sharp object beneath a bandage on his glove hand and give the ball a rough shave while he's rubbing it up.

As for scuffing, any abrasive substance will do. New York Yankees pitcher Whitey Ford has related how he wore a ring that was filigreed to the texture of a wood rasp. Sandpaper, emery cloth, and emery boards have found their way to the mound from the hardware store and manicure parlor. A roughened spot about the size of a quarter is all the scuff you need.

By the way, a ball needn't be cut or scuffed to have a sudden break. Even a splotch of mud will create the same aerodynamic irregularities. And it needn't be the pitcher who doctors the ball. Ford had his famous mudball prepared for him courtesy of catcher Elston Howard. Additionally, catchers have been known to scrape the ball against their shin guards, and certain Dodgers infielders of the 1960s were suspected of cutting the ball for certain Dodgers pitchers as it was tossed around the bases.

CORKED BATS

With all these trick deliveries in the pitcher's arsenal, not to mention the legal stuff, you would think the use of corked bats, as alleged, would be justifiable self-defense for batters.

I don't think that corked bats are used as a conscious counterweight to the perception that a pitcher might be doctoring the ball. It's merely an attempt by the batter to improve his performance, satisfy his ambitions, or solve his problems. For the guy with TP, or track power—the ability to hit fly balls out to the warning track—a corked bat might mean several more home runs.

This is to the extent that corked bats are used at all—and I don't believe the practice is widespread. The only major leaguer I know of who was candid about the fact was the late Norm Cash, who said he used a corked bat when he played for the Detroit Tigers in 1961 and won the American League batting title with a .361 average and 41 home runs.

There's a lot of voodoo involved with freak bats, both regarding how to load one and what the loading is supposed to achieve. From the woodworking angle, the magical formulas vary but are basically as follows.

A hole anywhere from 1 to $1\frac{1}{2}$ inches in diameter is bored through the fat end of the bat to a depth of about 1 foot. The wood that's been removed is replaced by cork (a dowel, beads, or rolled sheets) or bouncy Super Balls press-fit into the hollow barrel. Finally, the mouth of the hole is plugged with wood that matches the grain, and the top of the bat is stained and finished in a manner that camouflages the plug.

Why does anyone load a bat? One reason is to lighten it and thereby generate greater bat speed—the force with which the bat meets the ball. Another reason is bat control. If it takes less effort to bring the bat around, the hitter gains an extra fraction of a second to gauge the pitch before he commits to swinging.

Another thing some players believe is that the cork or rubber filling endows the bat with greater resiliency, making the ball jump off the bat with more pop. But science says it isn't so.

Los Angeles Dodgers player Wilton Guerrero was ejected from the game at St. Louis in the first inning on June 1, 1997, after breaking his bat on a groundout to second base. Dodgers manager Bill Russell (left) is shown the bat by home-plate umpire Thomas Rippley (right) as third-base umpire Bruce Froemming (center) looks on. It was found that the bat had been corked. Guerrero later admitted that the bat had been doctored. The Dodgers beat the Cardinals 6–1.

Lighter weight, not resiliency, is what makes the freak bat drive the ball farther. As Brancazio and others explain, the bat hardly deforms at all when it collides with the ball—or only hundredths of an inch if at all. But upon collisions, the ball deforms by an inch or two, squishing down almost to a hemisphere. So whatever you fill the bat with doesn't matter, as long as it is lighter than wood. And cork, according to Brancazio, has about one-third the density of wood. Super Balls give almost no weight savings at all. But something stiff and light like Styrofoam would work well too. Actually, a hollow bat would work best—if the hitter could be confident that the bat would hold up and not sound too hollow to the nearby catcher and umpire. In fact, Brancazio says that the newer-style cupped bats, the ones with an inch-deep scoop of wood removed from the business end, achieve the same effect in bat speed as boring out several cubic inches of wood farther down the barrel. That's because the mass, or weight, is removed farther away from the bat's pivot point at the handle. The net result is a lower polar moment of inertia when the hitter begins to swing.

What's the net result on the scoreboard? In his Tulane University lab, Watts has calculated that a hitter using a 32-ounce bat generates a bat speed of about 70 mph. If termites or other activity shed six ounces from this weight, bat speed rises about 2.5 percent to about 72 mph. The extra velocity, says Watt, translates into fifteen to twenty feet more mileage for the ball if it collides with the bat.

BACKSPIN IN A HIT

Meanwhile, another revelation from Watts's lab almost makes the point of corking the bat irrelevant. It has to do with the role of backspin in making a ball travel farther.

When a ball is propelled so the seams turn into the airflow, or against it, from the bottom of the ball to the top, it's said to have backspin. This orientation creates the force known in aerodynamics as lift. The more rpm in the spin, the greater the lifting force.

The way to give backspin to a batted ball is to undercut it with the swing. If you undercut the pitch too much, you pop up. Watts tells us that the optimal launch point is an area five-eighths to one inch below the equator of the ball. The difference between this uppercut and hitting the ball dead-center (so that it hardly spins) could, depending upon the angle of the swing, put as much as several thousand rpm of backspin on the ball—good for about 250 feet more travel. With just a small increase in backspin, the ball would travel another 30 feet.

Smart hitters have always sensed this, and Watts believes that more batters are becoming savvy to it. He points out that the amount of backspin is affected by the amount of friction generated when the bat strikes the ball. Applying a substance such as pine tar to the hitting surface of the bat would increase friction, but this is illegal. Something players used to do years ago was scrape out the dark-grained areas of the wood—in effect scoring the bat's surface in a manner resembling the face of a golf club—where the grooves are intended to impart backspin to the ball.

Although scuffing and corking are called cheating, I really don't agree with the term. Professional baseball players are more or less evenly matched. Everyone knows what is at stake, so I don't believe that taking an edge is cheating in the moral sense. Ballplayers call it gamesmanship.

All things being equal, I really think the trick pitches and freak bats ought to be legal. After all, let's look at some practices that are never questioned, or just winked at, but which give someone an edge.

THE LEGAL ADVANTAGES

Home teams routinely groom the field to give themselves an advantage, or put visitors at a disadvantage. The baselines get beveled to make bunts go fair or foul. The area in front of the plate can be watered down to favor a sinkerball pitcher, or hardened to cause Baltimore chop–type infield hits. Teams regularly soak the base paths or dump sand around first base to slow down base stealers. There are no strictures against any of this in the rulebook. At the time when I played for the Minnesota Twins, the Chicago White Sox used to store the baseballs in a freezer to deaden the ball. When our power hitters made contact, it was like hitting a rock and the ball didn't go anywhere. While we're at it, let's not forget about stealing the signs, or the way hitters stand behind the boundary of the batter's box to get a longer look at the pitch, or how a first baseman plants a foot in foul territory when setting up for a pickoff throw. And how a New York team (Yankees) moved its fences closer to its batters.

All of these things fall into the category of getting an edge. It's not as though they're criminal acts. And no matter if the book says they're legal or not, I don't think we'll see any less of them in the years to come.

TOP TEN CORKERS

[1] **SAMMY SOSA,** Chicago Cubs. Caught on June 3, 2003. Places a shadow on the 600-plus home runs hit over his career.

[2] **NORM CASH,** Detroit Tigers. Confesses after his retirement to using a corked bat in 1961 when he hit 41 HRs and 132 RBIs and led the American League in batting with a .361 average.

[3] **AMOS OTIS,** Kansas City Royals. After retiring in 1984, the five-time All-Star admits to using a doctored bat through much of his career.

[4] **GRAIG NETTLES,** New York Yankees. On September 7, 1984, Super Balls pop out of his broken bat. Nettles is not punished, and his previous home run is allowed to stand as the Yanks win 1–0 over the Detroit Tigers.

[5] **ALBERT BELLE,** Cleveland Indians. On July 15, 1994, a suspicious umpire confiscates Belle's bat. After the game, a teammate switches bats, but the subterfuge is spotted and Belle gets a seven-game suspension.

[6] **CHRIS SABO,** Cincinnati Reds. On July 29, 1996, umpires catch Sabo with a corked bat, but he denies it is his bat. Sabo gets a seven-game suspension.

[7] **BILLY HATCHER,** Houston Astros. Nabbed on August 31, 1987. He claims to have borrowed the bat from a pitcher. Hatcher gets a ten-day suspension.

[8] **WILTON GUERRERO,** Los Angeles Dodgers. Caught June 1, 1997. Guerrero admits his guilt and gets an eight-game suspension.

[9] **MIGUEL OLIVIO,** catcher on Chicago White Sox double-A minor-league team. He gets a six-game suspension in 2001.

[10] **JOSE GUILLEN,** triple-A minor leaguer in Devil Rays system. Guillen admits error of his ways and gets a ten-game suspension in 2001.

CHAPTER 3

Basketball

NOTHING BUT NET: MAKING THE 3-POINT SHOT

by BUZZ "THE SHOT DOCTOR" BRAMAN

This article was published in POPULAR MECHANICS in 1994.

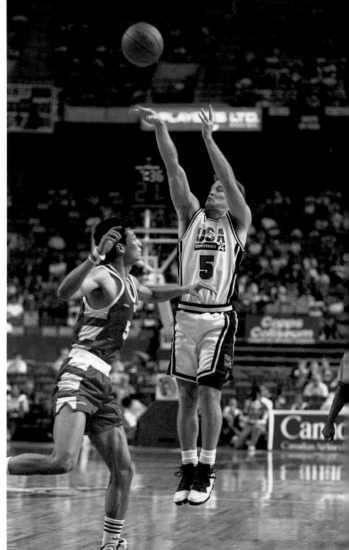

FOR A BASKETBALL PLAYER, THERE'S NO BETTER FEELING THAN SEEING A SHOT SWISH THROUGH THE BASKET. WHETHER IT'S AT THE BEGINNING OF THE GAME, AT THE BUZZER, OR FROM OUT IN 3-POINT LAND, MAKING BASKETS IS THE ESSENCE OF THE GAME.

Mark Price of the Cleveland Cavaliers was among the NBA's best ever 3-point shooters. In 1993 and 1994, Price won the 3-point shooting contests held prior to the All-Star Game.

To be a complete offensive player, a consistent jump shot is a must. Hot-and-cold shooting is a product of mechanical flaws in the stroke. In many respects, a 3-point shot is the same as a free throw since, mechanically, the shots are the same. The difference lies in the speed at which the shot is taken. A free throw is shot at whatever speed you want to shoot. A 3-pointer is shot at the speed the game dictates.

Shooting has become a lost art. In the past twenty years, the game has shifted toward athleticism. The National Basketball Association (NBA) and athletic shoe companies are marketing the dunk. Instead of practicing shooting, young players spend their time practicing the "slam." However, the growing importance of the 3-point shot—put up from 22 feet and beyond in the NBA—is now making good shooters a premium.

The NBA game has evolved into a game of double-teaming the superstar—someone like Shaquille O'Neal. When the ball is passed out of the double-team in the low post underneath the basket, the result is an open jump shot or an open 3-pointer. If more players could shoot the 3, there would be no more double-teaming. Zone defenses would be a thing of the past.

DIFFICULTIES OF THE 3-POINTER

So why is it so hard to shoot the 3-point shot?

The two biggest excuses for poor shooting are lack of confidence and lack of concentration. These are the standard answers given by coaches, players, and parents. What they don't realize is that lack of confidence and concentration are the effect, not the cause. When the ball doesn't go in, confidence and concentration slide.

But the real reason that the ball isn't going in consistently is poor mechanics. When the mechanics get straightened out and the ball starts going in the basket, guess what happens to a player's confidence and concentration?

All young players are taught several lessons about shooting that are important. You should "square up," meaning your shoulders and feet face the basket. You should also bend your knees for power and concentrate on the target.

These things are important, but let's face it, these are things most players do naturally.

The two biggest reasons for poor shooting are not being able to make the ball go straight consistently and not being able to judge distance correctly. What does this mean? It's really very simple.

There are only four ways to miss a shot: left, right, short, or long. If you could shoot a 3-pointer using a computer, all you would need to do is draw a straight line from the middle of the release, your fingertips, to the middle of the rim, which would be adjusted for the correct amount of thrust and arc for the ball to go the correct distance.

To be a consistent shooter, you must understand how to shoot straight and how to accurately judge the distance to the basket. Otherwise, you're shooting by instinct, and this leads to streaky shooting.

PROPER HAND PLACEMENT

For simplicity's sake, let's assume everyone is right-handed. To start, hold out your arm fully extended and with your fingertips spread. Look down your forearm as though you were looking down the barrel of a rifle. If you draw a straight line down your forearm to your fingertips, you will notice that only two of your fingers are within that straight line: your index and middle fingers.

Now hold a ball in your right hand as if you were going to shoot the ball. The shape that is formed from your wrist to your elbow and from your elbow to your shoulder should look like an L. When you make the L, it should be brought in front of you so that the straight line created by your forearm and extending up to your index and middle fingers is lined up toward the middle of the basket.

The shooting motion is an exercise in simplicity. From the L position, we bend our knees, thereby lowering the L. Then we simply push up. When the ball rolls off the fingers, guess which two fingers touch the ball last?

That's right. It's the index and middle fingers. The very last finger that touches the ball is the index finger. The miracle of straightness is this: wherever your index finger points when you release the ball and follow through is where the ball goes. When you push up under the L, your elbow locks straight and your wrist breaks. If your index finger is pointed over the middle of the front rim, the ball will never miss right or left. Since the rim is a circle, you can always see the middle of the rim no matter what angle you shoot from.

1.

2.

3.

4.

5.

⚜ **Shoot and Freeze:** The L-shaped shooting arm rises so the line from the forearm through the index and middle fingers lines up toward the basket. Freeze the follow-through until the ball reaches the basket.

1. The index and middle fingers of the shooting hand point toward the basket.

2. As the body elevates, the ball begins to roll off the fingers.

3. The left hand, fingers pointed upward, falls away from the ball.

4. Aim your index finger over the front of the rim and release the shot.

5. Follow through with the wrist bent over and fingers pointing downward.

Meanwhile, the correct amount of arc on the shot will be determined by three factors: the natural upward push motion of the L; your instincts; and freezing the follow-through at the point of release—when your arm locks straight and your wrist flips over—at a spot about six to eight inches above the rim.

So what is your other hand—the left hand in this instance—doing? Its job is very simple. A ball should be shot with only one hand. The left hand is just for support.

For a right-handed shooter, the left hand should be placed on the side of the ball at about the nine o'clock position. As the L moves forward, the left hand loses contact with the ball when the ball is level with your forehead. All five fingers of the left hand are straight up and down. The arm is bent and the palm faces to the right.

The left hand is not allowed to shoot, push, flick, twist, or face the basket. If it does, you are shooting with two hands.

What's so bad about shooting with two hands? If the palm of your left hand starts rotating toward the basket, then you are pushing the ball to the right and off the index and middle fingers. Remember, the ball goes where the index finger is pointing. Missing right or left is the result of the left hand pushing the ball. This is a very common mistake for players of all ages.

GOOD FOLLOW-THROUGH

Most players rely solely on their instincts and "feel" when it comes to judging distances. These are important considerations but not the only ones. The follow-through is a critical element as well. As it happens, follow-through is a phrase every basketball player has heard but which few can define.

The follow-through forms as the L of your arm rises, the arm locks straight, and, as the ball is released, the wrist finishes bent over with the fingertips pointing downward. After shooting the ball, you should freeze in this position like a statue, and don't move until the ball reaches the basket. This is the correct follow-through. When you have the same release and structure on every shot, you can then use your instincts and "feel" to a greater degree. Simply put, the method is shoot and freeze.

To better understand the importance of the follow-through, try this experiment. Stand at the foul line and, with the L formed, push up. As you shoot, jerk your arm back as fast as you can. You'll find you have no control over the ball.

Next, shoot and freeze. You now have maximum control over the direction of the ball.

Championship Shot:
Dallas Mavericks guard
Steve Nash (right)
launches a 3-point shot
over Portland
Trailblazers forward Dale
Davis that proved to be
the game winner of
Game 2 in the NBA
Western Conference
quarterfinals at the
American Airlines
Center in Dallas, April
23, 2003. Note the
follow-through.

"Pulling the string" is the phrase used to describe that jerking motion of pulling your arm back before you've finished the follow-through. Imagine there is a string connecting your index finger to the ball.

PRACTICE, PRACTICE, PRACTICE

The high school and college 3-point shot is 19 feet 9 inches. I once did a shooting demonstration at Villanova University for the Philadelphia 76ers' coaching staff and about twenty rookies. I shot 250 college 3-pointers and made 246. I made the first 92 in a row. I could hear the players' amazement as I shot.

What they didn't realize was that my mechanics were perfect: a perfect L shape of the arm, a perfect shoot-and-freeze motion, and a perfect left-hand release. Every ball I shot went straight.

Of course, they also wanted to shoot 3-pointers like that. But something else they didn't realize was that I shot 300 3-pointers a day for six months, training for that exhibition. Don't think that you can practice shooting a 3-pointer, or any other shot for that matter, by shooting only a few shots per day.

Practice does not make perfect. Perfect practice makes perfect.

To master the 3-point shot or any other shot, you need to practice it so many times it becomes second nature. It must become ingrained in your mind. Muscle memory is the key to becoming a good shooter. Even if your team is down by 2 points and there is only 1.5 seconds left in the game, when you pull up for the 3—assuming your technique is correct and you've prepared with long hours of practice—the only sound you'll hear before the crowd begins to roar will be the sound of your 3-point shot swishing through the net.

SLAM DUNK!

by PETER BRANCAZIO

THE SLAM DUNK
INVARIABLY BRINGS A
BASKETBALL CROWD
ROARING TO ITS FEET,
AND, MORE OFTEN
THAN NOT, THE
PLAYER MAKING THE
SHOT WILL FOLLOW
IT WITH A FIST PUMP
OR SOME OTHER
DISPLAY OF SELF-
CONGRATULATION.
BUT JUST HOW
IMPORTANT IS THE
SLAM DUNK AS AN
OFFENSIVE WEAPON?
IS IT GREAT
BASKETBALL OR
JUST SHOWMANSHIP?
HOW MUCH SKILL IS
REQUIRED TO BE A
SUCCESSFUL DUNKER?

A prolific scorer like
Kobe Bryant of the Los
Angeles Lakers may be
known for his outside
shooting, but he can
throw down a dunk with
the best of them.

TYPES OF DUNKS

The scientific study of any phenomenon normally begins with the
description and classifications of its forms. In this case, careful
observation reveals that slam dunks actually fall into a relatively
simple set of categories. The basic slam dunk begins with the
shooter getting the ball on a pass or rebound within three feet of
the basket, requiring, at most, one step to get to the hoop. The ball
may be delivered one-handed or two-handed with varying degrees
of force, ranging from a gentle dropped-in dunk to a resounding
two-handed overhead slam.

The next level of dunkmanship is the alley-oop. In this play, the
player catches a pass in midair above the rim and jams it home.
Requiring unspoken communication between passer and receiver,
an accurately thrown pass and a well timed leap and reception by
the jumper, a perfectly executed alley-oop is a thing of beauty.

The take-it-to-the-hoop or flying slam dunk represents an even
higher level of skill. Here, the player must move horizontally as
well as vertically, and the shot must be taken off the dribble. (In a
game, the player is allowed to take two steps between his last
dribble and the takeoff for the shot.) This move calls for good
acceleration and quick, instinctive body movements in addition to
great leaping ability.

The last and most spectacular variety is the freestyle slam dunk.
Here, the player is not required to dribble the ball or face a
defender, so his performance is limited only by physical skill and
imagination. A player can show off moves that he rarely gets to
use in a game because they are too bizarre, too difficult, or just
plain illegal. The best freestyle dunks involve an amazing array of
windmills, double-pumps, 360s, tomahawks, and the sometimes
unnameable.

HISTORY OF THE SLAM

The slam dunk was unknown in the early days of basketball.
Many of the players of the 1940s and 1950s were quite capable of
dunking the ball, but to do so was to invite retaliation, either by
having your legs taken out from under you on the way down or by
getting whacked later on the elbow or forearm when the referee

Wilt Chamberlain:
At 7-foot-1, Wilt
Chamberlain's agility
and unstoppable dunks
put him in the NBA Hall
of Fame.

wasn't looking. In those prehistoric days, a slam dunk was considered an insult that had to be answered.

The entrance of Wilt Chamberlain into the NBA in 1959 represented a key evolutionary turning point. At 7-foot-1, Wilt could dunk the ball easily, and it soon became his calling card. With his great physical strength and remarkable agility for a man of his size, Chamberlain was virtually unstoppable. Even the best defenders could only hope to deny him position under the hoop once in a while.

The slam dunk's rising popularity was due to the founding of a rival professional league, the American Basketball Association (ABA), in 1967. In an effort to attract fans, the new league emphasized a more wide-open, offensive game. The greatest star of the ABA was Julius Erving, who, with his huge hands, could hold a basketball as if it were a grapefruit. Whether in the open court or on a fast break or in the half-court against one or more defenders, Dr. J's graceful, soaring moves to the hoop redefined the standards of the slam dunk. Erving's signature move was his tomahawk dunk, in which he brandished the ball overhead—arm fully extended—as he approached the hoop. With the merger of the two leagues in 1976, Dr. J was able to bring his game to a nationwide audience.

Today, nearly every NBA player can slam-dunk, and the move has become almost commonplace. Virtually every team has one high-flying dunker. Names like Clyde "the Glide" Drexler of the Portland Trail Blazers and Karl "the Mailman" Malone of the Utah Jazz were among the marquee players known for their astonishing dunks. The list of great dunkers is a long one. However, it is generally recognized that to this day, only players of the caliber of Michael Jordan of the Chicago Bulls and Dominique Wilkins of the Atlanta Hawks have surpassed Erving in terms of spectacular mind-bending moves.

THE PHYSICALITY OF THE DUNK

What are the physical requirements needed to be able to dunk a basketball? The obvious requirement is, of course, that you have to be able to get the basketball over the edge of a ten-foot-high rim. This, in turn, calls for a combination of body height and jumping ability. It is also extremely helpful to be able to palm—grip securely with one hand—the ball. While it is not impossible to dunk the ball if you can't palm it, the variety and creativity of your dunks will be limited.

As a minimum requirement, you have to get your wrist to rim level in order to dunk the ball. This means that the sum of your standing reach and vertical leap must be 10 feet 6 inches or more. Your standing reach is essentially the distance from the floor to the tips of your fingers when you are reaching upward from a standing position. Using some basic observations about human anatomy, we can devise an approximate formula that relates vertical reach to body height. The length of a person's arm is about half the distance from his shoulder to the floor. If we take a person's body height in inches (H), subtract the distance from the top of the head to the shoulder (about 12 inches on average), and then add back half of this distance (about one arm's length), we arrive at the formula $R = 3(H-12)/2$, where R is the individual's standing reach in inches.

The difference between your vertical reach and 10 feet 6 inches—the minimum height that must be attained for a successful dunk—must be made up by jumping. For example, a 6-footer with a standing vertical reach of 7 feet 6 inches must have a vertical leap of at least 36 inches to get into dunking range.

What constitutes a good vertical leap? The average playground basketball player has a vertical leap of about 18 to 24 inches. Anything in the range of 24 to 36 inches is considered unusual, and any vertical leap over 36 inches is considered exceptional. The best vertical leap ever recorded for a basketball player (as of 1991) is 48 inches, set by Darrell Griffith in 1976. In the history of the NBA, probably only a handful of players have had vertical leaps exceeding 42 inches. Most of the great acrobatic dunkers, like Jordan and Wilkins, are in the 36-to-40-inch range.

If you would like to know what your own vertical leap is, you can measure it fairly easily. Just stand facing a wall, extend your arm upward, and make a mark with a pencil or piece of chalk. This is your vertical reach. Now jump vertically as high as you can, making a second mark on the wall. The difference between the two marks is your vertical leap.

Given the size and athletic ability of any hoopster good enough to make it to the NBA, or even for that matter to any top-ranked Division I college team, we should not be overly impressed by anyone 6 feet 6 inches tall or more being able to dunk. All that's needed is a fairly ordinary leaping ability. It's far more impressive to see someone dunk a ball when he is 6 feet 3 inches and has a vertical leap of 30 to 33 inches.

Given this criterion, perhaps the most amazing dunker of recent years is not Jordan or Wilkins, but none other than Spud Webb of the Atlanta Hawks. Listed at 5 feet 7 inches tall, Webb has a vertical leap in the 42-to-45-inch range. Or consider David Thompson, who played for the Denver Nuggets in the 1970s and

Spud Webb:
It's not always how tall you are but how high you can jump that counts. Even though he was only 5-foot-7, Spud Webb of the Atlanta Hawks had a vertical leap of between 42 and 45 inches. Likewise, David Thompson stood 6-foot-4 as a player for the Denver Nuggets, but a vertical leap of 42 inches allowed him to extend a foot and a half above the rim.

1980s. Standing 6 feet 4 inches, with a vertical leap of 42 inches, Thompson was capable of lifting a basketball a foot and half above the rim.

To players and fans alike, the great slam dunkers appear to be airborne for seconds at a time and seem to hang in the air almost at will. In truth, their flight times are surprisingly short. According to the laws of physics, an athlete's hang time depends entirely on his upward speed at the moment of takeoff and cannot be extended once he is airborne.

In fact, hang time and vertical leap are mathematically related. The formula relating the vertical leap V (measured in inches) to the hang time (measured in seconds) is V = 48 squared. According to this equation, a vertical leap of 48 inches translates to a hang time of exactly one second. A 36-inch vertical leap corresponds to a hang time of 0.87 second. As unbelievable as it may seem, the great high flyers in the NBA perform their greatest moves in the space of eight- and nine-tenths of a second. No small part of Michael Jordan's greatness was the fact that he seemed to cover great distances in the air. He accentuated this illusion by releasing his shots on the way down, rather than at the peak of his trajectory.

WHY THE EXCITEMENT?

Clearly, it's not a big deal for almost any NBA player to dunk a basketball. So why are fans so excited by the sight of 7-foot players jamming one down? And why do players get so turned on by what for them is really not a difficult accomplishment?

It's easy to see why the fans are so impressed. After all, the act of dunking a basketball is far beyond the capability of the average spectator, who is as likely to dunk the ball as he is to set foot on the moon.

As for the players, they are all large, well-built individuals, capable of acts of great physical strength. Yet shooting a basketball almost always requires a soft touch, calling for a carefully modulated and rather gentle application of force rather than an explosion of brute strength.

Slam-dunking a basketball is perhaps the only opportunity a player ever gets to really unload in a game. To be able to break through the confines of a tight pressure defense, to get close enough to the basket with the ball in your hands, and to go up and over a tough defender and throw the ball down through the hoop with as much force as you please just plain feels good. When a great player unloads, it can be both intimidating and inspiring.

HIGH FLYER

Basic

Alley-oop

Flying

Freestyle

Michael Jordan of the Chicago Bulls is widely acknowledged as the game's premier slam dunker, as well as among the best players ever to play in the National Basketball Association. Jordan had an arsenal of dunks at his command. Yet they basically fell within four classifications. As seen in the accompanying photographs of Jordan (from left to right, top to bottom), there is the basic slam dunk from a standing position, the alley oop dunk off a pass, the flying slam dunk after spinning through defenders, and the freestyle slam dunk.

The freestyle dunk is the most instinctive and creative of moves to the basket. Jordan himself didn't know what he was going to do until after his feet left the ground. Good elevation and the ability to shoot while on the way down contributed to Jordan's seeming ability to defy the laws of gravity.

While freestyle dunking is perhaps the most visually exciting, the powerful flying slam dunk is perhaps the most devastating since it signals a serious breakdown in the opposition's defense.

CHAPTER 4

Bowling

STRIKE FORCE

by JOHN G. FALCIONI

IN SPORTS LIKE
PROFESSIONAL FOOTBALL,
SUCCESS COMES AS A
DIRECT RESULT OF SIZE,
STRENGTH, AND SPEED.
SHOULDER PADS AND
HELMETS PROVIDE
SAFEGUARDS AGAINST
INJURY, BUT IN TERMS OF
PHYSICAL ATTRIBUTES,
EQUIPMENT CANNOT
IMPROVE WHAT MOTHER
NATURE HAS BESTOWED.
IN BOWLING, WHERE
STRENGTH IS NOT
ESSENTIAL TO GOOD
PERFORMANCE, BUT
NEVERTHELESS PLAYS
AN IMPORTANT ROLE, A
SERIES OF EQUIPMENT
DEVELOPMENTS HAVE
LEVELED THE PLAYING
FIELD FOR KEGLERS OF
ALL SIZES.

◀ PBA bowling champ
Patrick Healey Jr.
is a textbook stroker,
throwing the ball
with medium
revolutions and hook.

Today, the combination of a resin ball and the proper arm swing can make a 110-pound bowler rattle the pins as hard as a 200-pounder. Moreover, the revolutionary developments behind bowling's new wave of balls promise to free the sport from the shackles of a reputation created by the likes of Ralph Kramden and Archie Bunker. The sport has become so sophisticated that knowledge of engineering and physics is likely to prove more helpful in throwing strikes than doing curls with a dumbbell.

BOWLING-BALL UPGRADES

But in a sport big on tradition, where equipment upgrades such as the use of polyester in addition to rubber in a ball took decades, the sudden introduction of intricate core configurations for bowling balls and new reactive materials for their outer shells have been met with some criticism and a lot of confusion.

Many standout bowlers are critical of these balls (which are often called "cheaters"), arguing that players of lesser ability and striking power are now ranking among the top of the Professional Bowlers Association (PBA) prize-money list. This may be an overstatement, but it is true that even among amateurs the new balls are having a staggering effect. The American Bowling Congress (ABC) in Greendale, Wisconsin, reported that the number of perfect games—occurring when a player rolls twelve strikes in a row for a 300 score—soared to a national high of 17,654 during the 1992–93 winter bowling season, the first full season following the introduction of resin balls, versus 14,889 the previous season.

Introduction of the resin balls has even forced the ABC, which regulates the sport, to issue new guidelines that stymie manufacturers from illegally manipulating specifications such as a ball's coefficient of friction, coefficient of restitution, moment of inertia, and radius of gyration.

Essentially, resin bowling balls provide the two most important factors that increase the probability of striking: greater angle of entry into the pocket and greater energy transfer. Polished, these balls skid straight through the "heads," the oily first 45 feet of the lane, and then snap strongly in the "back end," the last 15 feet.

Resin balls produce significantly lower friction than traditional high-friction urethane balls, especially on the oily part of the lane, says Daniel Speranza, a mechanical engineer and manager of the equipment-specifications department at the ABC. But on the drier end, near the pins, resin balls appear to have higher friction than regular urethane balls. This results in a greater angle of impact into what's known as the "pocket"—for right-handers, the area on a lane between the headpin and the No. 3 pin, or between the headpin and the No. 2 pin for left-handers. In general, a greater entry angle to the pocket produces more strikes.

What makes these balls react so drastically on dry lanes is a heavily guarded proprietary chemical recipe. Manufacturers say that resin balls are created the same way existing urethane balls are made, except that the resin additive is mixed in. Bowling-ball makers have aligned themselves with chemical suppliers who concoct resin formulations for different companies. For example, the giant chemical supplier BASF Corporation developed a product with the trade name Versathane for a ball called Nuke, designed by Texas-based Track Inc.

THE CORE SHAPE

What differentiates balls of similar cover stock is the shape of the inner core. Brunswick Corporation, one of the world's leading producers of bowling equipment and supplies, is recognized as having taken the first serious foray into the core of the ball to predict reaction and consistency, the hallmark of good bowling performance. With its Phantom family of urethane balls, introduced in late 1991, Brunswick showed how the size, shape, and location of the core in a ball chiefly determined its rotation and reaction as it travels through and across the oil pattern on a lane.

Knowing how a ball is supposed to react, if released correctly, is important because, like different greens on a golf course, bowling lanes vary greatly. In fact, the oil pattern of even a single lane will change several times during a game, causing the ball to react one way during the early frames and differently by the end of the game. The reason for this is the shifting of the oil used to condition the lanes. A mineral oil is applied to all lanes once a day to protect the wood from the pounding of the balls. Typically, the first 25 to 40 feet of a lane are oiled, with a heavy concentration applied to the middle of the lane and a medium concentration on the outside edges.

The number of balls rolled on a lane will change the lane conditions, and so will the temperature inside and outside the

Resin-Ball Weight-Block Designs

Lightbulb

Spherical

Elliptical

bowling center. Therefore, a lane condition will change even if no one is bowling on it because of the evaporation of the oil. That's why predicting how a ball will react is essential to consistency.

"The shape of the core is significant in predicting reaction because it provides the dynamic stability to maintain the preferred axis of rotation after drilling the grip holes," says Ray Edwards, an engineer and former professional bowler who became a research and development specialist at Brunswick.

Bowling balls are produced in two or three pieces depending upon the desired effect. Traditional three-piece balls provide a controlled and "true" roll. These balls feature a weight block of two to four ounces added to the core during manufacture. The block compensates for the weight that is removed by drilling the grip holes. Two-piece balls consist of a single-piece core and the cover stock. These balls generally begin to roll earlier on the lane than three-piece balls. Missouri-based manufacturer Faball Inc. is credited with developing the two-piece ball, now the favored construction method.

The cores themselves are made of a resin system and high- and low-density fillers. A good example of the new breed of bowling ball was a triple-density ball produced by Track Inc. called Critical Mass, which features a distinctive heavy ceramic circular core inside its regular lightbulb-shaped core. The ball is topped off with the same Versathane cover stock used in the company's Nuke ball.

"This ball is capable of generating the lowest radius of gyration possible to achieve maximum revolutions with less hand action," says Phil Cardinale, president of Track. The hard ceramic core of the ball was designed to begin rolling on the oily part of the lane, as a urethane ball does, and then, because of its resin shell, react sharply in the back end of the lane. By not skidding through the oil, this ball was designed to provide the advantage of a urethane roll with the power of a resin ball. (Radius of gyration measures how the mass and density of a ball are distributed. A ball with a higher radius of gyration will travel in a straight path for a longer period of time.)

Critical Mass was innovative because it was the first to use a heavy ceramic core. Meanwhile, Brunswick even started a new company called Quantum BTV (Brunswick Technology Venture) that quickly introduced three new balls. These Quantum balls, says Bill Wasserberger, an engineer in the R&D department, preserved the rotational dynamics of 15- and 16-pound balls in lighter weights (10, 12, and 14 pounds). Each ball, regardless of weight, is designed to have the same maximum and minimum radius of gyration for a standard roll. The company is doing this by varying the shape of the core of each ball, within the same family, depending upon its weight.

Generally, ball weight affects reaction on the lanes. If you roll a 16-pound ball and a 12-pound ball with identical core shapes on a lane, the 12-pound ball will "hook long" or go straighter longer and make its break to the pins later. The Quantum balls were designed to react or break the same way regardless of weight.

CRANKERS VERSUS STROKERS

When it comes to releasing the ball, there are as many styles as there are bowlers. But among professionals, there are two basic methods: the power swing or the traditional swing. Many pros stick closely to one or the other, while most amateurs mix and match.

Resin balls allow strokers, accurate bowlers who lack a powerful strike ball, to "blow out the rack" with the best of the crankers. Despite his 6-foot-2-inch frame, 1993's hottest bowler and top money winner, Walter Ray Williams Jr., was considered a stroker. By using Ebonite's Crush/R resin ball for his first shot in most of the bowling tournaments that year, the 33-year-old transformed the reaction of his ball into that of a cranker's. He was able to strike consistently on light hits to the pocket that would have left pins standing were he using a non-resin ball.

For crankers, or big-hook bowlers, however, resin balls have not had a major impact on their scores. Take unlikely power bowler Chris Warren. His physique is reminiscent of a Charles Atlas "before" photo, yet the 5-foot-4 $^1/_2$,

"STROKER" DELIVERY

"CRANKER" DELIVERY

The rendering shows a comparison between a right-handed "stroker" and a "cranker," each using a five-step approach. From left to right, the stroker (top) pushes the ball out in front of him in the second step, has a level backswing by the fourth step, and releases the ball smoothly during the sliding fifth step. To gain added leverage and power, the cranker (above) will open his right shoulder during the third step, as if to throw a roundhouse punch. By the fourth step, the ball will be above his shoulder and ready for a quick swing. At the point of release, the arm will snap up abruptly toward the head. The cranker's wrist will be cocked throughout the arm swing.

115-pound Texan throws the ball as hard as anyone on tour—118 mph.

Warren says he's always been a cranker. The keys to his success are foot speed and arm swing, which create momentum and leverage. Warren's foot speed, uncommon for many short players, allows him to raise his right arm quickly on the backswing. At the top of his swing, Warren opens his shoulder to gain the leverage necessary for a quick follow-through.

Additionally, power bowlers like Warren cup their wrist when releasing the ball so the ball rotates more, resulting in greater ball impact when it hits the pins. The final step occurs at the point of release, when a quick upward bend of the elbow produces what's known as lift on the ball. Lifting the ball complements cupping the ball in creating rotation.

Accuracy and consistency were keys to Brian Voss's success. Voss, winner of thirteen PBA titles and more than $1.2 million in his twelve-year professional career, is a cross between a cranker and a stroker. At 5-foot-10, his picture-perfect style generated the consistency to make him a perennial money winner. He too uses a resin ball.

"You cannot not use a resin ball these days. I'd be losing ten pins per game if I didn't use them," Voss says, "and that's too much when you have guys hitting the pocket with these balls."

For better or worse, resin balls have changed the game for good. In 1992, resin balls were perceived as a fad, but now they have become a mainstay, says Jim Mailander, president of the Maryland-based ball manufacturer Champions Bowling Products Corporation. "People thought the resin-ball popularity would die. If that's true, it's been one of the longest wakes in history."

Resin-Ball Track:
Because a resin ball (red line) will skid through the "heads" of the lane and hook sharply into the pocket, the ball is released farther inside on the lane. Thus, when the ball begins hooking to the "pocket," the angle of impact will be greater that that of a non-resin ball (blue line).

Boxing

THE KNOCKOUT PUNCH

by WILLIAM J. HOCHSWENDER

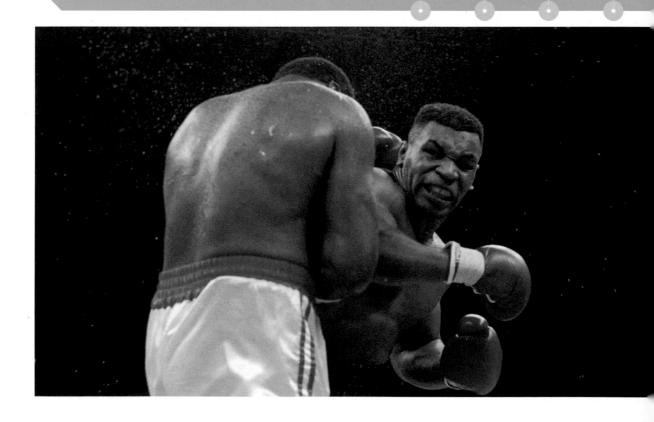

EVER SINCE THE
ROMANS CONQUERED
THE GREEKS AND
CHANGED BOXING
FROM AN HONORED
MILITARY DISCIPLINE
INTO A BLOOD
SPECTACLE FOR THE
ELITE, THE KNOCKOUT
HAS BEEN THE GOAL
OF THE SPORT. IT IS
ONE OF THE FEW
OCCASIONS IN ANY
ATHLETIC CONTEST
WHERE SYMBOLIC
CONQUEST AND REAL
CONQUEST MERGE. IT IS
A KIND OF DEATH THAT
RARELY BECOMES REAL.
IT CAN BE SUDDEN
AND CATEGORICAL—
10 SECONDS IN
DREAMLAND FOR THE
LOSER, ABSOLUTE
VICTORY FOR
THE WINNER.

◀ Mike Tyson, a famous
practitioner of the
knockout punch, plying
his trade on the jaw of
fellow heavyweight
Larry Holmes during the
fourth round of the
World Heavyweight
Championship in 1988.

It can also be disturbing.

One thinks of Mike Tyson's 1986 first-round onslaught against
Marvis Frazier, in which a rapid-fire sequence of uppercuts had
Frazier's senseless head jerking and bobbing eerily atop his
powerful frame. Or the 1988 Tyson–Larry Holmes finale, where
the once dominant former champion was smashed into a dazed
state before succumbing to a punch that snapped his head back
violently and sent him flopping to the canvas like a lifeless doll.

Both of these climaxes illustrate important biomechanical and
medical points about the nature of the knockout itself—how a
fighter loses consciousness, why some boxers are bigger punchers
than others, what constitutes a glass jaw, and so on. However, even
when it comes to the brute force of the boxing ring, a knockout
punch is so subtle and complex that it not only eludes our senses
but baffles the understanding of scientists. The so-called sweet
science still holds its mysteries.

THE MYSTERY OF BOXING

Certainly boxing, like most other sports, can be appreciated on
many levels. The first-time observer at ringside will see and
appreciate a much different prizefight than a veteran fan, or even
an ex-boxer or trainer. Boxing insiders convincingly offer bits
of wisdom that challenge the most educated conclusions of
physicians.

Ray Arcel, who trained twenty world champions, from Barney
Ross and Tony Zale to Roberto Duran and Larry Holmes, believes
the knockout will always defy analysis. "I've seen guys go down
from a light tap and not move," he says. "Of course, generally, there
has to be some power behind the blow, but it's not how hard you
get hit, but where and when you get hit. I don't think anybody can
ever explain that."

Arcel cites the example of Jim Braddock, whom he trained to
defend his heavyweight title against Joe Louis in 1937. "Braddock
went out in the first round and hit Louis on the chin and put him on
his back. No one could believe it because he wasn't a puncher. But
he could take it. He had been hit harder by guys with more power
and he'd survived. But then when Louis hit him, he went down."

Arcel also recalls a strange episode in the career of Ezzard Charles. In the 1940s and 1950s, Charles was a great boxer as a heavyweight champion, and no one could knock him out—not even Rocky Marciano, who fought him to a bloody decision. But in the last round of one of Charles's four fights with Jersey Joe Walcott, he got hit with a punch, Arcel remembers, "that could've knocked a wall down. Charles lasted out the round, but the punch, a left hook, left an impression."

The next time the two fighters met, the unstoppable Charles was stopped in the seventh round, flattened by a punch that came out of nowhere and which, Arcel believes, was a carbon copy of the punch he had earlier survived. "He just knew somewhere in his mind that it should have knocked him out."

BEHIND THE KNOCKOUT PUNCH

Technically, a knockout punch is simply a form of cerebral concussion. It results in either unconsciousness or a groggy state that makes it impossible for the boxer to rise from the canvas or continue. According to Dr. King Liu, a sports-medicine researcher at the University of Iowa Medical School, "A concussion can be defined as a dramatic loss of consciousness caused by a disruption of the neurons in the reticular formation in the brain stem."

This means that when a blow is delivered to the head, it causes a variation—what Liu calls a high-pressure gradient—between the brain and the spinal cord, a twisting and tearing of the regulatory cells (neurons) that results in a shutdown. In other words, the jawbone sends a message to the brain: go to sleep.

Barry D. Jordan, medical director of the New York State Athletic Commission, divided the knockout into four categories of severity. In Type I, the boxer is dazed and unable to defend himself—out on his feet. This commonly results in a technical knockout. Type 2 is when the boxer is knocked to the canvas and cannot rise before the count of ten, yet remains conscious. In Type 3, the fighter is knocked unconsciousness but recovers quickly. Type 4 involves a longer period of unconsciousness.

CAUSE OF THE KO

Jordan, who published original research on the neurological aspects of boxing, is a student of the knockout. "Basically, what causes the KO is a rotational acceleration, a spinning of the brain," he says. "Picture the brain as, say, a mushroom or a cauliflower. During a knockout, the stalk doesn't move, but the spin at the top causes you to lose consciousness. That's why headgear won't prevent KOs. It doesn't preclude the acceleration."

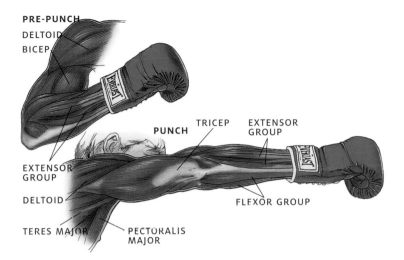

PRE-PUNCH
DELTOID
BICEP

EXTENSOR
GROUP

DELTOID

TERES MAJOR

PECTORALIS
MAJOR

PUNCH   TRICEP   EXTENSOR
GROUP

FLEXOR GROUP

A knockout punch can begin at the feet, ripple through the torso and culminate with a complex interaction of several muscle groups in the arm.

Professional boxers can deliver blows with such force to the movable head that the brain smacks against the skull, tearing nerve fibers, the meningeal sac that supports the brain and blood vessels. The direction and power of the blow determine the severity of this tearing.

There are two basic kinds of acceleration: rotational (or angular) and linear (or translational). The former tends to be caused by roundhouse punches or hooks, the latter by straight shots. According to Dr. Jordan, linear acceleration, caused by a punch that sends the head straight back, is not as likely to cause a KO. But, as he points out, "Obviously, the right amount of force can cause a KO: it depends upon where it is applied."

Referring to the Tyson-Holmes bout, Jordan observes that the first knockdown, a right to Holmes's temple—an example of linear movement—did cause acceleration. It left the former champ rubber-legged and uncoordinated—a Type I state.

A groggy fighter who has lost control of his neck muscles, as Holmes had, becomes even more vulnerable to sudden rotational acceleration. Thus, the final punch—maybe not as powerful as the first—a sweeping left uppercut to the point of the chin, rapidly swiveled Holmes's head, resulting in a Type 3 knockout. It's important to note that the severity of the punch in the Tyson-Holmes fight example is not the issue. The punch that flattened Holmes was hardly the kind of haymaker one associates with a knockout. The video replay indicated a lightning-quick poke to the chin, followed by Holmes's head snapping, and a somewhat graceless collapse to the mat—reminiscent of a falling tree.

Here, it is worth mentioning that even a straight punch causes

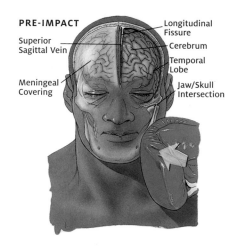

PRE-IMPACT

Superior Sagittal Vein

Meningeal Covering

Longitudinal Fissure

Cerebrum

Temporal Lobe

Jaw/Skull Intersection

▲ The brain, meninges, and attendant blood vessels reside within the protective shell of the skull.

some degree of rotational acceleration. As Dr. Jordan has written, "In reality, the distinction between a punch that causes a purely rotational or linear acceleration is mostly theoretical, because the force produced by the blow is usually some variable combination of linear and rotational acceleration."

The linear component and the rotational component—individually or in concert—are the root cause of the knockout. And when these two dynamic boxing elements merge and mix, the mystery of the knockout only deepens.

OTHER KO FACTORS

There is one last type of acceleration, or rather deceleration, to be considered. This is not caused by punches but by the impact of the fighter's head on the canvas. The collision between the brain and the skull on rapid deceleration only aggravates the effects of rotation of the brain within the skull, and can lead to bruises on the brain's lobes.

Knockouts have also been known to result from injuries to the carotid, the chief artery passing up the neck to the brain—usually from a very powerful blow to the neck, which compresses the carotid sinus, deprives the brain of oxygen-carrying blood, and causes shock and injury to the cerebrum.

And then there are body punches. As Arcel observes, "I've seen boxers who could absorb a terrific amount of punishment get tapped in the solar plexus and go facedown."

PUNCHING POWER

So what makes a Louis or a Tyson so devastating a puncher? Moreover, what makes a physically unimposing boxer a knockout artist? And what makes one fighter better able to withstand a big blow than the next guy? Is there such a thing as a glass jaw?

As is well known to anyone who's had his fair share of fights, there are guys built like Arnold Schwarzenegger who couldn't KO a dandelion, and there are scrawny dudes who can flatten a truck with one shot. The mystery of punching power is elusive.

As Jackie Graham, former deputy commissioner of the New York State Athletic Commission, points out, George Foreman and Gerry Cooney are both known as arm punchers, fighters who don't maximize the force of the blow by using their bodies for leverage. Yet both somehow succeeded in knocking out most of their opponents—and quickly. Foreman and Cooney belie the notion that punching power must be truly forceful to achieve a knockout. While a Joe Frazier or a Mike Tyson can accomplish knockouts by planting their feet and rotating their entire bodies

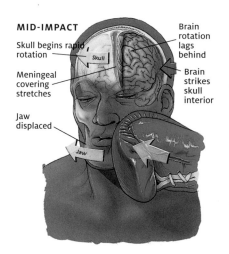

MID-IMPACT

Skull begins rapid rotation

Meningeal covering stretches

Jaw displaced

Skull

Jaw

Brain rotation lags behind

Brain strikes skull interior

▲ A blow to the head begins a rapid rotation of the skull, bruising the brain and meningeal covering.

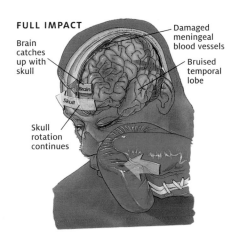

FULL IMPACT

Brain catches up with skull

Skull rotation continues

Damaged meningeal blood vessels

Bruised temporal lobe

Brain

Skull

⬥ Rotation of the brain relative to the brain stem and the collision of the brain with the skull result in a knockout.

behind the force of a blow, arm punchers seem to knock out their opponents with feathery quickness.

Graham remembers Lew Jenkins, a great lightweight champion of the 1930s: "He had hands the size of a little girl's and pipestem arms, and he was drunk half the time. Yet he could punch like a mule. It has to do with accuracy, direction, leverage, and who knows what else. As for durability, take my brother, Billy Graham. He fought 120 fights—and he was in with Sugar Ray Robinson, Carmen Basilio, Joey Giardello—and he was never even knocked down!"

POWER PRINCIPLES

Nevertheless, certain classic principles apply. As Dr. Jordan has written in the *Archives of Neurology*: "The concussive properties of a boxer's punch relate to the manner in which the punch is delivered and how the mechanical forces are transferred and absorbed through the intercranial cavity...The force transmitted by a punch is directly proportional to the mass of the glove and the velocity of the swing, and is inversely proportional to the total mass opposing the punch."

In essence, these are Newton's second and third laws. At the most basic level, the force of the punch is computed by size or mass of the gloved fist times its speed (force = mass × acceleration). But since we are discussing two bodies in motion, we must also consider that the force of the glove on the head is equal and opposite to the force of the head on the glove. This resistance of the head and neck to the effect of rotation must be considered when calculating the ability of a boxer to take a punch.

Newton's third law comes into play most intriguingly in the technique known as rolling with the punch. Many clever boxers, notably Muhammad Ali, diminish the impact of the blow by abruptly pulling back their head at the instant of collision—rolling with it, so to speak. In this manner, skull and brain accelerate more in unison, thus diffusing the damage of the blow.

It is easy to see, therefore, that a sudden, unexpected punch that catches a fighter unprepared, his jaw hung like a lantern, can result in a tremendous acceleration of the head. The soft brain, which does not move as fast as the skull itself, is deformed, with resultant stress to, and even tearing of, nerves and blood vessels in the brain's protective meninges.

An additional biomechanical factor is the duration of contact. According to Dr. Liu, "Relatively low-magnitude blows with a long contact period can do the same job as a more forceful punch. A good analogy is found in karate. In trying to break a stack of bricks with a blow of your hand, you might discover that in the split second the force applied reaches a certain level and the pain in your hand is intense, you would withdraw, but a karate master maintains contact until the bricks are broken. A good boxer, in the same sense, follows through."

As to why some fighters can absorb more punishment than others, says Dr. Liu, "Individual variations in the way brains are constructed enable some people to sustain a higher brain pressure gradient—or rotational acceleration—than others. It's simply part of the variation in all of nature."

Do some boxers suffer from the so-called "glass jaw"? Ray Arcel contends that the term is nothing more than "a newspaper expression."

"We never used it," Arcel explains. "Certain areas, certain nerve centers, in some individuals, may be more susceptible to a punch. In my own experience, certain guys were made of sterner stuff than others. Let's face it. The human body was never made to be punched."

True. But since the advent of this primordial sport, the human body has absorbed and delivered countless blows. Perfecting the knockout punch has been and always will be the ultimate goal in a competition mixing skill and toughness with what professional boxers know as an inner, indefinable fire.

CHAPTER 6

Cycling

THE FASTEST HOUR

by DEAN GOLICH *and* CRAIG GRIFFIN

THE TOUR DE FRANCE, A THREE-WEEK-LONG RACE THROUGH FRANCE THAT COVERS 1,800 TO 2,500 MILES (3,000 TO 4,000 KM), IS THE MOST FAMOUS CYCLING EVENT IN THE WORLD, BUT PERHAPS EVEN MORE PRESTIGIOUS IS AN EVENT THAT RECEIVES LITTLE FANFARE. IT IS CALLED THE HOUR RECORD, AND IT IS WHERE TOUR DE FRANCE VETERANS HISTORICALLY HAVE COME TO PROVE TO THEIR COLLEAGUES THAT THEY ARE INDEED THE WORLD'S BEST RIDERS.

Lance Armstrong discovered that the power requirements for riding in a circular velodrome were much different than those needed for the hills and valleys of the Tour de France.

The Hour Record is the longest distance cycled in one hour, and the event takes place in a velodrome, an arena specifically built for track cycling.

HISTORY OF THE HOUR RECORD

The connection between the Tour de France and the Hour Record dates back to the inception of both races. An Hour Record of 21.95 miles (35.325 km) was set in 1883 by Henri Desgrange, founder of the Tour de France. Since then, a legion of cyclists has assaulted the Hour Record. By July 2005, Czech Ondrej Sosenko had increased the Hour Record to 30.882 miles (49.7 km).

In many respects, however, the most important date in the Hour Record is 1972, when Belgian cycling legend Eddy Merckx logged 30.71 miles (49.422 km) in what was then a new record. Merckx's record was surpassed in subsequent years but only through the use of radically reconfigured bicycles that relied on advances in technology. To put the emphasis back on the athlete and not on technology, the sport's governing body, the Union Cycliste Internationale, instituted a technological freeze on the Hour Record in 2000. Bicycles used in the Hour Record must be configured and could not be lighter than 12.68 pounds—the weight of the bike used by Merckx in 1972. Ironically, Sosenko achieved his Hour Record utilizing what some might consider an unforeseen loophole: Sosenko's bicycle was heavier than Merckx's. No maximum weight limit had been set in the rules, and Sosenko found that once the heavier bike had been brought up to speed, it was easier to maintain.

LANCE AND THE HOUR RECORD

The best cyclist of his generation is unquestionably Lance Armstrong, who won the grueling Tour de France seven times. The question, therefore, is what would have happened if Armstrong had attempted to break the Hour Record? In 2005, a team dubbed the F-One Group met to consider the hypothetical question. The team consisted of Carmichael Training Systems, which oversaw Armstrong's training, aerodynamics specialist Len Brownlie, and representatives from a long list of equipment suppliers and sponsors that included Trek, Nike, Giro, Hed Cycling, and AMD.

Among the first questions to be addressed was the location. Armstrong has never ridden competitively in a velodrome, so it was clear that a period of acclimation would be necessary. A typical velodrome is between 250 and 330 meters (about 825 to 1,100 feet) long. You're also riding at an angle. A 250-meter track has a 45-degree pitch on the curves and a 15- to 20-degree pitch on the straightaways.

In a velodrome, the application of power at the proper time makes all the difference. Power increases on the straightaways and decreases on the turns. At the same time, you have to be conservative in your application of power to avoid unwanted spikes in the application of power to the pedals. Unlike the Tour de France, the Hour Record is done in a single, fixed gear.

PEDAL POWER

Power is the benchmark that you train by. Power is measured as torque and then converted into watts by a power meter. Training with a power meter allows you to see what's happening on a bike in real time as it travels over distance.

As you might expect, the power requirements for the Hour Record are different than those for the hills and valleys that constitute the Tour de France, where you are using most of your effort to overcome the force of gravity. What's important for climbing is your power-to-weight ratio. The ideal weight for a climber is less than two pounds of body weight per inch of height: a light rider has less weight to carry up the hill than a heavier one. What's important in the Hour Record is your power-to-surface-area ratio. Given the proper surface area, weight, and aerodynamic data, you can predict how much speed is required to cover a specific distance. If the goal is to surpass about 31 miles (50 km) in an hour, for example, then the required lap times can be deduced, as can be the necessary power requirements. The latter becomes a tangible training mark. But this computation is not as simple as it first appears because you are not accelerating across a straight line. You are going more slowly through the curves and then accelerating on the straightaways. In effect, you're doing four intervals every lap. The power requirements also oscillate more frequently on a shorter track and less so on a longer track.

So now we're faced with a new set of questions. How much power can a rider produce? How much power do you need to break the Hour Record? And lastly, how much does power production vary depending on altitude and other environmental conditions?

ENVIRONMENTAL CONSIDERATIONS

There was no doubt from the beginning that if Lance Armstrong were to attempt the Hour Record, he would do it at a high altitude, probably in Mexico City. While there is less oxygen in this location—this causes a 6 to 8 percent drop in performance—it is offset by a 16 percent reduction in drag due to the thinner air density. On balance, then, you wind up with at least an 8 percent improvement in performance at a high altitude. The tricky part is in the training: you don't want to train excessively at high altitude because you decrease your ability to produce maximum force. At the same time, you have to train at altitude in order to perform well. Striking the right balance between the two is hard work. This is also where the physiology of the athlete becomes a big variable.

In many respects, the Hour Record is all about drag reduction. Aerodynamic resistance accounts for 90 percent of the retarding force on a cyclist. Bicycle components—clothing, shoes, helmet, wheels, tires, and frame—are tested in wind tunnels, and every effort is made to reduce drag in their manufacture. Things get more complicated at the track, however, because of varying wind angles. This is where rider position becomes critical. The trade-off here is aerodynamics versus power. Is the rider flexible enough to lower his aerodynamic profile to reduce drag while still maintaining maximum power out in that position? We may be able to reduce a rider's frontal resistance by positioning alone, but he may be able to produce more power in a less aerodynamic position. (The bike itself accounts for 20 to 25 percent of the frontal surface area.) Does a 1 percent improvement in aerodynamics mean the rider is going to produce ten percent less power, for example? Again, physiology becomes a big factor. A lot of times, a rider can hold an ideal aerodynamic position for ten or fifteen minutes, but an hour becomes a true test of a rider's mettle.

BODY FACTORS

Body type also becomes a consideration. In the Tour de France, cyclists tend to be small, and this generally translates into an increased power-to-weight ratio. The Tour de France is won going uphill. In the Hour Record, total weight is not as much an issue as is total frontal surface area. You can be a tall, skinny rider as long as you're flexible enough to get into a good aerodynamic position. Conversely, a tall, skinny rider may do poorly in the Tour de France, where carrying weight uphill is an issue.

Another difference between the two events is the regulation of your core body temperature. In the Hour Record, you can't bring anything with you to drink. Some athletes are better able to cool themselves than others. Competitors in the Hour Record often will engage in some type of pre-cooling before the attempt to get their core body temperatures down because the amount of heat you generate adversely affects the amount of power you can generate.

LANCE'S TRAINING

For the recreational rider who wants to increase distance during a defined workout period, the training plan for Lance Armstrong may prove illuminating. Basically, we used interval training. Assuming that Armstrong would have to produce 400 watts of power in an hour to cover a specific distance, we started with an overall target of 45-to-50-minute workouts at 430 watts. Then we would section those minutes into ten-minute workouts with a recovery time of five to eight minutes. As training progresses, we would lengthen the cycle time and shorten the recovery period, making sure the power level is about 10 percent above what would be required to break the Hour Record. By training at 430 watts for 45 minutes, we hope for 420 watts when it comes time for the actual attempt at the Hour Record. A complicating factor is rpm. Armstrong can pedal 100 rpm without a problem. This means he can sustain more power than someone who can pedal at only 90 rpm and has to use more force per pedal stroke to maintain the power requirement. There are only two ways to increase speed: pedal harder or pedal faster.

CRUSHING THE RECORD?

Would Lance Armstrong have broken the Hour Record? Remember, historically speaking, crushing the Hour Record means breaking it by approximately 15 or 30 feet (5 or 10 meters), basically a body length. Unless he decides to try, we'll never know the answer for sure, but we think he would. That view is supported by Dan Heil, a sports physiologist at the University of Montana. Heil, whose work appeared in the *European Journal of Applied Physiology*, predicted that Armstrong would have smashed the record. Heil's mathematical model of the rider's physiology and the external forces on the bicycle and the cyclist showed that Armstrong would have broken the Hour Record by almost 1.25 miles (2 km), a feat that would have made the Hour Record probably untouchable for decades.

We can only dream about what might have been.

LANCE'S BODY

A key factor in Lance Armstrong's success is that he may not have a body like most of us, thanks to a combination of training and good genes. According to an article published by *The Science Channel*, Armstrong's muscles, heart, and lungs all work at levels superior to those of the average person. In addition, after beating cancer, Armstrong lost twenty pounds but was still able to generate the same amount of power. This increased his power-to-weight ratio by 10 percent, a significant edge in a sport where races can be won by a 1 percent margin. Here are the key body parts that made Armstrong an extraordinary athlete.

MUSCLES: For some unknown reason, Armstrong's muscles produce less lactic acid than average, and he has an ability to eliminate lactic acid more efficiently as well. And according to the Human Performance Laboratory at the University of Texas at Austin, Armstrong apparently over time increased the number of slow-twitch muscles in his body by 20 percent. Slow-twitch muscles do not burn out as quickly and are used in standing or walking. This means that Armstrong can maintain full power longer than his rivals.

HEART: Armstrong's heart is a third more effective than average, pumping nine gallons of blood per minute at maximum output as opposed to the average of five gallons. During that same minute, Armstrong's heart will beat 200 times.

LUNGS: The average young man can extract 45 millimeters of oxygen from the air with each breath, while Armstrong extracts 83 milligrams. With this extra oxygen, Armstrong can generate 500 watts of power compared to an average of 250 watts.

Lance Armstrong's body is anything but average. His lungs have twice the capacity of an average man, and a longer-than-average femur bone in his thigh lets him apply extra torque to the pedals. His body fat while competing was typically between 4 and 5 percent, while the average is 16 percent.

To go as fast as possible in one hour, Team Discovery made modifications to the bicycle to make it as light and aerodynamic as possible. Here are the key changes:

SEAT: The seat mast has an airfoil shape like a plane's wing to reduce drag.

FRAME: Air-foiled shape.

BARS: Low profile helps reduce wind resistance and also forces the rider to adopt a stretched-out position to further reduce drag.

TIRES: Tubular tires have a special casing that holds the inner tube and is attached to the rim of the wheel with special glue. Tires are pumped to 130 to 140 pounds per square inch for races.

FRONT WHEEL: Spokes have an airfoil design.

BACK WHEEL: A flat disk provides more stability and also allows air to flow around the frame for better aerodynamics.

WEIGHT: Minimum weight required by Union Cycliste International is 14.96 pounds.

CHAPTER 7

Football

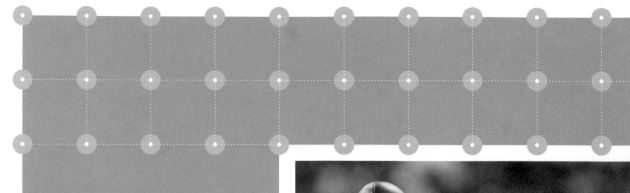

THE
MECHANICS
OF THE
BOMB

by JOHN BAKKE

FOOTBALL MAY BE A GAME OF INCHES, BUT A LONG PASS—THE BOMB—TAKES THEM BY THE THOUSANDS, BREAKING THE SPORT'S GROUND-ATTACK PATTERN IN A SINGLE LONG-DISTANCE GAMBIT. IT'S FOOTBALL'S SLAM DUNK, ITS HOME RUN. NOTHING ELSE CAN ACCOMPLISH SO MUCH SO QUICKLY OR WITH SO MUCH EXCITEMENT.

Quarterback Peyton Manning of the Indianapolis Colts was named MVP of Super Bowl XLI.

Part of the play's drama is its all-or-nothing style, but those who know best insist the bomb is more craft than crapshoot. Indeed, its success relies on timing and coordination from the players, as well as smooth and accurate lofting of a ball not particularly suited to easy flight.

INTRICACIES OF THE PLAY

For the football strategist, precise timing is the key. "It's far more important than arm strength," says Don Shula, the Hall of Fame coach who led the National Football League's (NFL) Miami Dolphins to a perfect season in 1972 and amassed 347 wins between 1963 and 1996.

The play's development actually can be faster than passing plays, covering less distance. With the need for quickness, the quarterback customarily drops back only five steps, instead of the usual seven. In that time—just three to four seconds—the receiver has moved downfield ten or fifteen yards and is just coming alongside the player defending him.

This is a crucial moment in the play, in two regards.

First, the receiver must be positioned to move past his defender and stay ahead of him the rest of the way. If he isn't, the critical timing is destroyed. If he is, the rest of the play is an all-out sprint for another 30 to 35 yards to where, if all goes well, the ball will be waiting for him.

Second, the pass itself must be launched to near perfection, possibly with defenders closing in. The quarterback must throw to a spot some 50 yards away, where the intended receiver will not be for another four to five seconds. The margin of error may be only one yard in either direction.

Quarterback Dan Marino is one reason why Shula's Dolphins led the NFL in 1987–88 with an average of nearly 260 passing yards per game.

"Like any passing pattern, timing is essential," says Marino, whose NFL records for most career touchdown passes (420), most career yards (61,361), and most career passes completed (4,967) stood unchallenged for many years.

As delicate a feat as it seems on the field, throwing an accurate bomb is even more remarkable when considered in a mechanical context. Spin, angle of attack, trajectory, and velocity all combine to bring a football into the hands of its intended receiver.

THE BALL

The most significant consideration in a football's flight is also the most obvious—its shape. A football can present many different profiles to the air it sails through, with the forces governing its flight varying considerably.

"Aerodynamically, a football is a very unstable object," says Professor Pasquale Sforza, head of the aerospace engineering department at Polytechnic University of New York. "Baseballs and other spheres are very stable by comparison."

The fundamental effect of its oblong shape is a lack of stability, with a resulting need for spin, which creates a steadying gyroscopic effect.

To throw a good spiral, the quarterback must spin the ball around an axis that runs lengthwise through the center of the ball. If the spin axis is off, the pass will assume a drag-inducing wobble.

Assuming perfect spin, a football's angle of attack can still vary—that is, the position of its nose in relation to the trajectory, which is the same as the path traveled by the ball's center of gravity.

If the ball is at a positive angle of attack, with the nose above the direction of flight, air forcing its way over and under the ball will give it some lift, much like an airplane wing.

When air passes over any object, there is always some drag. For a football, the coefficient of drag can vary. From studies of a rotating projectile in axial flow (spinning the same way a football does), one might conclude that the drag coefficient would decrease with the speed of the spiral. Unfortunately for the quarterback, though, the spin would likely have to be well over 1,000 rpm, whereas the typical good pass is in the range of 600 rpm.

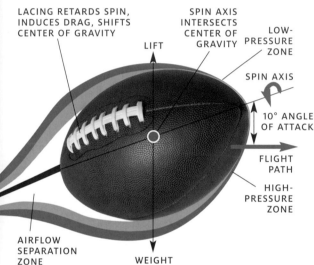

PRINCIPLES OF PIGSKIN AERODYNAMICS

LACING RETARDS SPIN, INDUCES DRAG, SHIFTS CENTER OF GRAVITY

SPIN AXIS INTERSECTS CENTER OF GRAVITY

LIFT

LOW-PRESSURE ZONE

SPIN AXIS

10° ANGLE OF ATTACK

FLIGHT PATH

HIGH-PRESSURE ZONE

AIRFLOW SEPARATION ZONE

WEIGHT

A spin-stabilized airborne football has reduced drag because of its elliptical shape. Extra-long yardage is gained when low-pressure airflow passing over the top of the football produces lift, just like an airplane wing. A perfect pass results when a football's spin axis maintains a 10-degree angle of attack relative to trajectory along its entire flight path.

Angles of Attack: Drag decreases with longer projectiles—like bullets and spinning footballs.

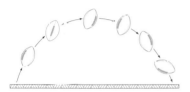

Pass Interference: The angle of the spin axis relative to trajectory widens in the later stages of flight, causing the ball to tumble.

Path to Completion: A true bomb maintains its 10-degree angle of attack for the entire length of the quarterback's intended flight path.

Velocity is a different story. The faster the ball travels, the lower the coefficient of drag. Curiously, for a sphere there is one range where the drag coefficient drops considerably with only a slight increase in velocity, so throwing just a touch harder will mean far less deceleration due to drag. For a football, there is no data to support a similar effect. But aerodynamicists think it might occur in the range of 40 to 45 mph.

Here too, the gyroscopic phenomenon brought about by the spin comes into play. Beyond basic stabilization, this effect maintains and self-corrects the ball's orientation. Consider a rising pass, the ball's nose pointed upward and its spin axis aligned ideally with the trajectory. As the ball ascends, reaches its apex, and starts to descend, the nose slowly continues to tip forward and ultimately points downward because—in the same way that a gyroscope resists disruption, or a top returns to its upright position when slightly disturbed—the football's spin acts to keep the spin axis and trajectory aligned, maintaining maximum lift and minimal aerodynamic drag.

ANGLE OF ATTACK

Not all passes gracefully turn over in this way, though. The passes that don't do so tend to be launched at high-trajectory angles and with overly positive angles of attack. The gyroscopic effect keeps the spin axis in a constant angle of inclination, and on descent the ball will assume an even greater angle of attack. With a far greater lift and torque than in an ideal orientation, the result is precession, or a wobbling, of the football's spin axis.

A great quarterback might very well instinctively also use factors such as angle of attack to control the ball's flight.

"These are things we might measure after a quarterback has developed his particular technique through trial and error," says Sforza. "For a great quarterback, minor adjustments in headwinds or tailwinds or crosswinds, or getting a little extra hang time by using a slightly greater positive angle of attack, are second nature, a subconscious talent."

CONTROLLING THE THROW

Considering the precision that a good pass requires, the football seems almost designed to resist throwing. To control spin and orientation, the hand needs to be close to the center of gravity, that is, near the ball's middle. However, to generate sufficient velocity the hand's force needs to come from behind, in other words, as far back as possible.

The resulting grip represents a compromise. A quarterback will hold the ball as far back as he can while still far enough forward to maintain control.

Throwing a football well requires the player to make a cumbersome object behave in a variety of ways. Beyond finding the right balance of direction and velocity, the quarterback must control spin and orientation. It's little wonder the experts rate the bomb high on a list of quarterback duties.

"The bomb is one of the most delicate passes a quarterback has to throw," said the late Sid Gillman, a coaching veteran of 27 collegiate and 25 professional seasons. "You've got to throw it not just with distance but also trajectory. It's got to be laid up there and timed perfectly."

Gillman worked for five NFL teams and was head coach of the San Diego Chargers for twelve years. Many consider him the pioneer of the passing game in the NFL, which inducted him into the Pro Football Hall of Fame in 1983.

"What you're doing, if you have a productive deep passing game, is stretching the field," said Gillman, who saw the long ball as both tactical and psychological weapon. "And I mean a productive game. Defenders start to worry about getting beat deep."

Both Gillman and Shula are careful to distinguish between the true bomb and plays that rely on a little bit of luck. For instance, the long, desperate play known as the "Hail Mary" can be mistaken for a bomb because it goes so far, but as a pass it is basically a heave.

"The bomb is tougher to complete, but the rewards are greater," says Shula. "A quick in or a quick out is easier to execute, but it gains under 10 yards. You can use it to keep your drive going. You hit the bombs and it's 50 or 60 yards and a touchdown." His quarterback agrees.

"I think a quarterback gets a feeling of excitement when the long bomb is completed," says Marino.

The beauty of football is its coordinated action, and the long pass is an impressive expression of just that—two players, widely separated, connecting their efforts with the high flight of a pass rising from the finesse to drop...just like a bomb.

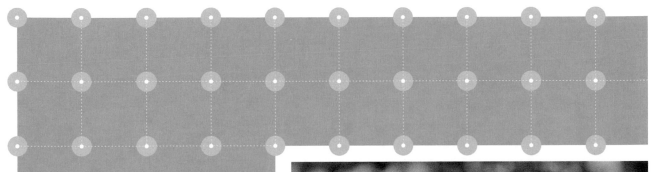

KICKING A
FIELD GOAL

by MATT BAHR

This article was published in
POPULAR MECHANICS in 1992.

ONE OF THE GREAT PARADOXES OF FOOTBALL IS THAT THE PLAYER WHO SPENDS THE LEAST AMOUNT OF TIME ON THE FIELD IS THE PLAYER WHO OFTEN DETERMINES WHETHER HIS TEAM GOES HOME A WINNER OR A LOSER AFTER THE GAME.

Kickers, it can be argued, may have become unintentionally prominent on the field, and perhaps some of the original spirit of the game has been lost due to the impact kickers can have on the outcome of a contest. As the game stands now, though, there will be many instances during the course of the season when all eyes will be focused on the kicker.

THE CENTER AND THE HOLDER

Yet a kicker is only one cog in a well-oiled machine that performs its job in 1.2 seconds. The other key elements in the equation are the center's snap, the hold, and the protection. Without these, there's no kick.

Centers are offensive linemen who can pass the ball like an upside-down quarterback and then be immediately blasted by a defender. For a field goal, the center snaps the ball backward seven to eight yards, depending upon the kicker's preference and how quickly he can elevate the ball. As the ball reaches the holder it should be still on the rise. The snap has to have pace, but it can't be hiked so hard that the holder has to fight to hold it. Most NFL

◀ Matt Bahr of the New York Giants kicks a field goal during Super Bowl XXV against the Buffalo Bills at Tampa Stadium in Tampa, Florida, in 1991. The Giants won the game, 20–19.

▶ Hungarian-born Pete Gogolak is credited with popularizing soccer-style kicking. Gogolak (Buffalo, 1964–65; New York Giants, 1966–74) led the American Football League in field goals in 1965.

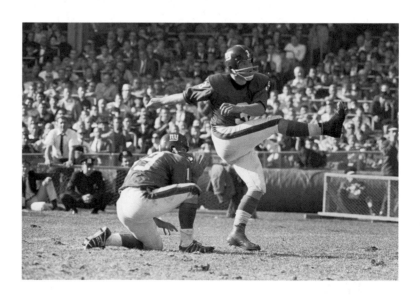

centers are able to snap the ball so that the laces are facing forward when it reaches the holder.

The holder, meanwhile, wants to meet the ball and bring it down with him. The best position in which to catch the ball is with the back knee up and the front knee down. In this position, the holder can move to the ball if the snap is off without getting out of position. The back knee acts as a backstop and also as a guide for positioning the ball. Holding the ball with the left hand (for a right-footed kicker) allows the holder to spin the ball laces forward if necessary with his right hand. The laces of the ball should always face forward—laces facing toward either side will make the ball curve in that direction. This also gives the kicker a good view of the ball. Quarterbacks tend to be the best holders because they handle the ball the most and have an even temperament. A calm holder keeps the kicker calm.

KICK STYLES

All NFL kickers use a soccer-style approach, meaning they come at the ball from a 45-degree angle. Soccer-style kickers dominate the league because they are more accurate than straight-on kickers. The accuracy comes from getting more of the foot's surface area on the ball. A soccer-style kicker hits the ball with a larger rectangular area of the foot, as opposed to a single point. Your foot also doesn't have to be angled as severely to hit the ball correctly.

One great exception, of course, is Tom Dempsey, formerly of the New Orleans Saints and holder of the record for the longest

Tom Dempsey of the New Orleans Saints walloped the ball for a record 63-yard field goal on November 8, 1970, against the Detroit Lions.

field goal at 63 yards. While Dempsey kicked straight-on, his club foot was like a war mallet, affording him plenty of surface contact with the ball (see photograph on previous page). Jason Elam of the Denver Broncos, a soccer-style kicker, tied Dempsey's record in 1998. Today, the only straight-on kickers in the NFL are emergency backup kickers who normally play other positions.

THE PLAY

Remember, the holder positions the ball seven yards behind the line of scrimmage, eight yards if the kicker drives the ball. The kicker assumes, however, that the offensive line will be pushed back two yards. This means the ball must rise ten feet—the height of a lineman with his arms extended upward—within five yards, or fifteen feet. Placing the ball farther back allows the world-class sprinter at the end of the defensive line to run in a straight line to block the kick. Forcing the defensive cornerman to run at the ball in a bow pattern slows him down. The idea is to get as far away from the line of scrimmage as possible without giving the defensive corner a line to run on. A fast defensive cornerman can run to the block point in 1.4 seconds. That's why you practice kicking in 1.2 seconds. At 1.3 seconds, a kicker is pushing the ragged edge. At 1.4 seconds, you eat the ball.

I start my move to the ball as soon as it hits the holder's hands. For me, it's two steps and a little hop to get the motion going. As I approach the ball, my supporting leg is planted a foot's length away from the ball. You should be able to draw a straight line from the ball to a point between the arch and the heel of the planted foot. The toes of the planted foot are pointed at the target, the target being some point through and beyond the goalposts. Your body weight is over the ball, and this puts you in position to maximize your follow-through.

Soccer-style kickers approach the ball from a 45-degree angle. The planted foot, which points toward the target, is a foot-length away from the ball as the kicking foot makes contact. The ball is kicked toe-down on the upper part of the shoelaces. A quick skip keeps the hips from turning. Forward momentum, therefore, stays directed at the target. Hips and shoulders are aligned toward the target during the follow-through.

The contact point is the football's sweet spot one inch below the center of the axis of the ball.

MECHANICS OF THE KICK

The best place to hit the ball is in the sweet spot just below the center of the ball. When I make contact, I'm hitting the sweet spot with the top part of my foot—on the shoelaces—with my toe pointing downward. The ball goes up, not because you're lifting it, but because you're hitting it just below the center axis.

For me to hit the sweet spot effectively, the holder should position the ball at about a 5-degree angle toward his body rather than straight up and down. Because of the angle at which your foot is hitting the ball, this slight tilt actually creates a more perpendicular alignment between the foot and the ball. This positioning reduces the tendency of the ball to hook off-target while it's in the air. Footballs hook when your hips and shoulders open up too much and your kicking foot comes across the ball.

Hitting the ball with the laces forward is ideal. Hitting the ball with the laces facing back is almost as good. Of course, with the laces back, you don't get the desired compression of the ball, because the laces are in the way. Laces facing to either side screw up the ball's rotation. With the laces to the side, the mass of the ball shifts, as does the position of the sweet spot.

Older balls are better to kick than new balls. With wear and tear, the ball becomes a balloon. It becomes easier to kick because there's more compression and it goes farther. In a game, every ball is new, but the home-team ball boys will give an official a ball that is a little less new than the others. The difference between kicking a new ball and an older ball may mean as much as an extra ten yards in distance. Every little bit helps.

As I'm planting my left foot, my kicking leg is already cocked—so much so that it looks as if I'm kicking myself in the back. The knee is bent at a 45-degree angle, and the lower portion of the leg is virtually parallel to the ground. By bending the knee and whipping your leg toward the ball, you get the foot speed necessary to kick the ball for distance. For a split second, neither of my feet is on the ground. My kicking leg has to be cocked before the other leg is planted because there is no time to do it any other way.

As I'm planting my foot, the holder is putting down the ball. During the kick, the lower back and the stomach muscles are moving toward the ball even before my foot is.

I'm more of a mechanical kicker than a natural kicker. This means I try to do the same thing every time whether it's a 45-yard field goal or an extra point. There are no chip shots.

The difference between a natural kicker and a mechanical kicker is most evident during the follow-through. A natural kicker

Kansas City kicker Jan Stenerud and quarterback Len Dawson watch as Stenerud's 48-yard field goal passes through the uprights during the first quarter of Super Bowl IV at Tulane Stadium in New Orleans, Louisiana, on January 11, 1970. The 48-yard kick was a Super Bowl record.

will add a little distance by turning his hips away from the target after contact. I work on taking my hips all the way through the kick. However, I stop my hips from turning and instead direct my momentum toward the target. At this point, I'm skipping through the ball and my left ankle looks as if it will break if I come down on it. The hop prevents me from spinning and keeps me aligned toward the target. This way, if I mis-hit the ball, the momentum of the follow-through still gives me a chance to make the field goal. By contrast, when a natural kicker mis-hits the ball, you'll see an audacious hook or a lot of rotation because he's under the ball or because it slid off his foot.

As a kicker, you want the ball to have a slow rotation. You can tell from the rotation where the ball was kicked. Hit the sweet spot and you'll see a slow end-over-end rotation. If the ball spins like a top, then the kicker has hit way under the sweet spot.

A KICKER'S ENEMIES

At one time, kickers had to worry about things like leapers—defensive players who took a running start from behind the line of scrimmage and then jumped into the air. Offensive linemen bet on whether they could make leapers do a 360-degree or 540-degree spin in the air. To prevent injuries, the defense is no longer allowed to jump from behind the line of scrimmage.

Today, a kicker's biggest adversary is the weather. Cold weather can cut your range by five to ten yards because you don't get as much compression of the ball as you kick. Wet weather forces you to shorten your stride to avoid slipping. The biggest problem, though, is the wind.

The wind can kill your kick, but you never want to choose a target that would take the ball on a natural trajectory outside the goalposts. The wind can die just as quickly as it starts up.

A wind coming straight at the kicker will kill the ball distance-wise, but it doesn't push the ball to either side. A wind coming from the left doesn't cause many problems because you're kicking through a cross section.

However, a wind coming diagonally from the right is murder because if you have any hook on the ball, the wind will exaggerate it—pushing the ball too far to the left. If you hit into the wind you won't get any hook, but you'll miss to the right. Under the circumstances, making an accurate kick is very difficult.

The wind does help if you have it at your back. You'll get about three-quarters of the range that you lose with the wind in your face.

Let's say I can normally make a 50-yard field goal. If a strong wind is in my face, it will reduce my range to about 40 yards. With the wind at my back, my range will increase about 7.5 yards, so there's a chance I will make a 57-yarder.

Adversity is part of the game, so it can't be offered as an excuse for a missed field goal. Kickers are always about three misses away from retirement. The key to longevity is to kick the ball in a natural and comfortable way with as much leg speed and accuracy as you can muster.

JUST ONE KICK IS ALL IT TOOK

by PETER BRANCAZIO

Since a football is not perfectly round, the aerodynamic forces influencing its flight depend significantly on the alignment of the football's axis with respect to its path toward the target.

For a field-goal kicker, getting the football to spiral nose first is impossible. The best alternative is to make it spin end-over-end around a side-to-side axis. While the aerodynamic drag is greater than it would be for a spiral, the ball will at least have a gyroscopic action, giving its spin axis a constant direction in space. On an ideal end-over-end kick, the spin axis of the ball should be horizontal and parallel to the yard lines as the ball

travels toward the goalpost. If there's no wind, the ball will not drift or curve sideways.

To achieve maximum distance, a field-goal kicker should launch the kick at about a 45-degree angle. To prevent the kick from being blocked, the ball should be at least ten feet above the ground two yards before the original line of scrimmage. This is ensured if the kick is launched at an angle of 35 degrees or more. Finally, the ball must be hit with enough force to clear the crossbar, ten feet above the ground. This means the actual landing point of the trajectory must be at least three or four yards past the goalpost.

Professional field-goal kickers are frequently called upon to perform this difficult task under exceptional pressure in the closing seconds of the game with a win—or even the championship—on the line.

One of the classic examples is Matt Bahr's 42-yard field goal that sent the New York Giants to Super Bowl XXV in 1991. Bahr's kick was straight and true, with a perfect end-over-end rotation, and with three seconds on the clock, the Giants defeated the San Francisco 49ers for the NFC Championship.

A close examination of the videotape showed that Bahr's kick cleared the crossbar by a considerable margin, landing about twelve yards behind the goalposts. Thus, the overall distance was about 54 yards. The hang time was 3.6 seconds. A computer simulation, taking the effects of air resistance into account, indicates the kick was probably launched with an initial speed of about 65 mph, at an angle close to 45 degrees.

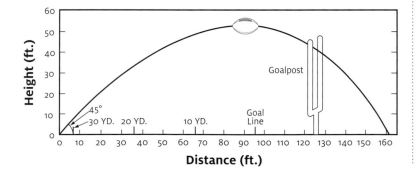

BATTLE HELMETS

by ANDREW GAFFNEY

WHEN YOU STRAP ON A FOOTBALL HELMET, PART OF YOU FEELS AS IF YOU'RE GOING TO WAR, LIKE SOME MEDIEVAL KNIGHT OF OLD ABOUT TO WAGE HAND-TO-HAND COMBAT. THE REALITY IS THAT FOOTBALL IS JUST A GAME, BUT ONE THAT COMES WITH THE RISK OF PHYSICAL INJURY. THAT'S WHY THE PLAYERS WEAR HELMETS.

It's no secret that quarterbacks Troy Aikman of the Dallas Cowboys and Steve Young of the San Francisco 49ers retired because of repeated head injuries. Their depature focused more attention on helmets and the need to further protect players against debilitating and life-threatening concussions.

In 2002, Riddell developed a new Revolution helmet designed to reduce the incidence of concussion. Schutt Sports Group, the other major helmet manufacturer, followed suit with an improved helmet of its own called DNA. A three-year, Riddell-financed study of high-school players by the University of Pittsburgh Medical Center found that the annual rate of concussion was 5.3 percent for players wearing the Revolution helmet and 7.6 percent for players wearing standard helmets.

While no helmet can prevent a concussion, these helmets offer a protection level that is unprecedented. It's been only 60 years since helmets were made mandatory in the NFL and in colleges. In fact, former President Gerald Ford was one of those players who braved the game without a helmet, in the early 1930s, as a center for the Michigan Wolverines. And while that opened the door for a lot of one-liners about the need for helmets, that little tidbit does illustrate how far head protection has come in the interim.

HELMET HISTORY

Although helmets did not become standard gear until after World War II, some pioneering players wore primitive head covering as far back as the early 1900s. The earliest versions, called "head harnesses," were made of soft leather and were predominantly designed to cover the ears. Because the flaps on the original head harnesses covered the ear completely, however, they were criticized for hindering communication on the playing field.

The first helmets offering full protection of the skull and featuring holes in the earflaps were introduced between 1915 and 1917. Although the flat-top caps were still made of soft leather, they offered some suspension, rather than resting directly on the skull.

During the 1920s and 1930s, makers began to utilize harder leathers and some fabric cushioning for greater protection.

Cincinnati Bengals and Indianapolis Colts players at the line of scrimmage prior to the snap during the game at the RCA Dome in Indianapolis, Indiana, in December 2006. The Colts defeated the Bengals 34–16.

Helmets also began evolving from the flat-top shape, adopting more of the teardrop shape of the skull and allowing the impact of a blow to slide to one side rather than being absorbed head-on.

BIRTH OF THE MODERN HELMET

The granddaddy of helmet innovation, however, came in 1939, when the John T. Riddell Company of Chicago introduced the first plastic football helmet. In addition to being stronger than leather models, the plastic helmet proved to be more durable. Riddell is credited with adding the first face mask, also plastic, in 1940 and moving the helmet strap from the Adam's apple to the chin.

Despite its performance improvements, the plastic helmet did have to overcome some hurdles before it would drastically change the game. Because plastics and other materials were scarce during World War II, some of Riddell's early models were not particularly well made. In fact, after Fred Naumetz of the Los Angeles Rams split nine in one season, plastic helmets were banned from the NFL. (Meanwhile, that same year, Fred Gehrke, another Rams player, and a former art student, became the first to paint a team logo on his helmet.)

Riddell quickly made some refinements in the types of synthetics used for construction, and with some lobbying from coach George Halas of the Chicago Bears, plastic helmets were reinstated in 1949 and soon after became the official helmets of the NFL. Riddell's earliest molded shells still serve as models for modern energy-absorbing helmets, which feature specially molded polycarbon plastic construction and high-tech cushioning systems.

Face masks evolved along the same lines—with early versions often shattering—until the development of the tubular bar in 1955. Popularized by legendary Cleveland Browns quarterback Otto Graham, the single bar soon blossomed into the vertical birdcage worn by today's players. Dark visors were added in the mid-1980s for use by players with eye injuries.

OTHER INNOVATIONS

While a number of innovations—including a one-piece system designed to replace the conventional helmet, shoulder pads, and rib guard—were proposed, one that stuck is the ProCap from Protective Sports Equipment, in Erie, Pennsylvania. The ProCap is basically a polyurethane semi-hard pad that attaches to the outside of a standard football helmet. Buffalo Bills trainer Ed Abramowski first recommended the pad to safety Mark Kelso in 1990 after he had suffered a string of concussions. Kelso went on to play five more seasons with the ProCap and became such a supporter of

Early 1900s
Soft leather harness style.
YMCA team from Latrobe,
Pennsylvania.

1915
Soft leather flat-top style.
Typical of early pro team
Canton Bulldogs.
YMCA team from Latrobe,
Pennsylvania.

1920s
Soft leather helmet.
Typical of the NFL's
Duluth Eskimos.

1930s, early 1940s
Hard leather style.
Typical of the NFL's
Chicago Bears.

1940s
Hard leather,
first graphics.
Los Angeles Rams.

1950s, 1960s
Plastic helmet.
Detroit Lions.

1970s, early 1980s
Plastic helmet.
St. Louis Cardinals.

1980s to present
Plastic helmet.
Minnesota Vikings.

Riddell Revolution
helmet.

ProCap, a polyurethane pad that attaches to the
outside of the helmet, is an added safeguard
against concussions.

 The Evolution of the Helmet

the product that he predicted it will "one day be the standard in the helmet industry." In addition to Kelso, Steve Wallace, an offensive tackle with the San Francisco 49ers, was an early adopter, wearing it in the 1995 Super Bowl. The product became widely used in youth, high school, and college programs.

ProCap was designed by Bert Strauss, a former industrial-design consultant, who saw the need for more protection from concussions and other head injuries. Strauss claimed that the ProCap absorbed 30 percent more energy than whatever helmet it sits on, reducing the impact and trauma to the head. Strauss compared ProCap to softer car bumpers.

Riddell and Schutt Sports Group still dominate the football helmet trade. Riddell's new Revolution helmet is the biggest structural change in helmet design in a generation. After research showed that 70 percent of concussions were the result of side impact, Riddell extended the helmet shell to cover the jaw area. The company also included an inflatable padding system for a more custom fit and used computer software to design the helmet around the head's center of gravity. The distance between the helmet shell and the interior pads was increased and the face guard was isolated to reduce jarring to the shell from face guard collisions. Fullback James Hodgins of the St. Louis Rams became the first player to wear a Revolution helmet, in Super Bowl XXXVI. Schutt responded with a new DNA helmet that uses a shock-absorbing plastic material called Skydex, the same material used to protect the heads of Army paratroopers and Navy SEALs.

The future may lie in radio telemetry. Numerous college teams are experimenting with Riddell's Head Impact Telemetry (HIT) System, which alerts sideline coaches when a preset impact threshold has been reached for an individual player. Six small sensors, similar to those that trigger airbags in cars, are inserted in the player's helmet. Impact data is transmitted wirelessly to a computer on the sideline.

Thankfully, there is no going back to the day when Ivy Leaguers grew their hair long to protect themselves from head injuries. Smart technology wins out over toughness, even on the gridiron.

ANATOMY OF A HIT

by MATT HIGGINS

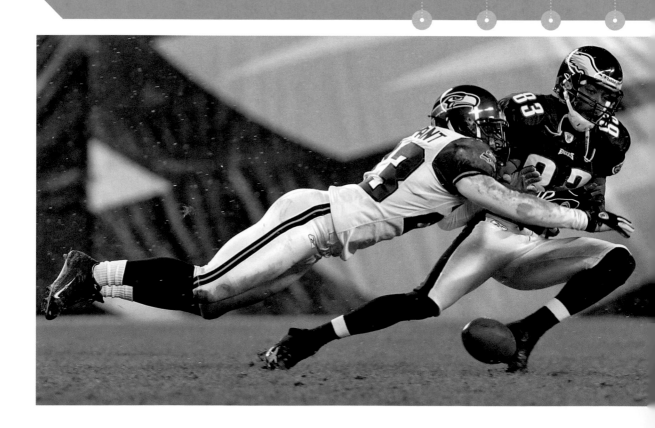

IT HAPPENS ABOUT 100 TIMES A GAME IN THE NATIONAL FOOTBALL LEAGUE: A BONE-JARRING TACKLE THAT SLAMS A PLAYER TO THE TURF. INCOMPLETIONS AND FUMBLES AREN'T THE ONLY CONSEQUENCES OF SUCH TACKLES— MORE THAN 100 CONCUSSIONS ARE RECORDED EACH SEASON IN THE NFL.

Given the size and speed of today's athletes, it's surprising that more gridiron warriors aren't carried off the field on their shields. For that, they can thank high-tech gear that protects them from the physics at play in the sport's fearsome collisions.

HALF A TON OF HURT

At 5-foot-11 and 199 pounds, the Seattle Seahawks' Marcus Trufant is an average-size NFL defensive back (DB). Those stats don't stand out in a league where more than 500 players weighed 300-plus pounds at the 2006 training camps. But a DB's mass combined with his speed— on average, 4.56 seconds for the 40-yard dash—can produce up to 1,600 pounds of tackling force, according to Timothy Gay, a physics professor at the University of Nebraska and author of *The Physics of Football*.

A tackle with more than half a ton of force sounds like a crippling blow. But, according to John Melvin, an injury biomechanics researcher for General Motors and NASCAR, the body can handle twice that amount—as long as the impact is well distributed. That job usually is handled by the player's equipment, which spreads out the incoming energy, lessening its severity.

BODY ARMOR

According to Tony Egues, chief equipment manager for the Miami Dolphins, shoulder-pad plastic hasn't changed much in 25 years, but it is now molded into designs with more right angles to deflect impacts. Players also rely on the helmet's solid shell and face mask to redistribute the energy of a collision.

During a tackle, foam padding beneath the plastic components of equipment compresses, absorbing energy and reducing the speed of impact. (The slower a hit, the less force it generates.) Visco elastic foam, which was invented by NASA to protect astronauts from g-forces during liftoff, retains its shape better than conventional foam, rebounding rapidly after hits.

According to a Virginia Tech study, a tackle like Trufant's in the photo at left probably caused Philadelphia Eagles receiver Greg Lewis's head to accelerate in his helmet at 30 to 60 g's. VT researchers gather data with the Head Impact Telemetry System,

◀ Seattle Seahawks defensive back Marcus Trufant (23) drilled Philadelphia Eagles receiver Greg Lewis (83) with such force that Lewis couldn't hang on to the ball. Seattle won the December 5, 2005, game at Philadelphia 42–0 in the most lopsided shutout ever broadcast on *Monday Night Football*.

which employs sensors and wireless transmitters in helmets. "We see 100-g impacts all the time," says Stefan Duma, director of the university's Center for Injury Biomechanics, "and several over 150 g's."

While Trufant and Lewis generally have enjoyed healthy careers, they (and other players) face the same nemesis: the dreaded knee injury. The knee's anterior cruciate ligament can withstand nearly 500 pounds of pressure, but it tears far more easily from side hits and evasive maneuvers. According to the *Pittsburgh Tribune-Review*, more than 1,200 knee injuries were reported by the league between 2000 and 2003, accounting for one out of every six injuries—by far the highest percentage in the NFL.

HITTING THE DECK

Researchers rate a field's shock absorbency with a metric called G-Max. To measure it, an object that approximates a human head and neck (about twenty square inches and twenty pounds) is dropped from a height of two feet. A low G-Max means the field absorbs more energy than the player. Trufant and Lewis landed on grass in Philly's new stadium, which has a cushy G-Max of just over 60. Synthetic surfaces have G-Max ratings of up to 120. The hardest turf: frozen grass.

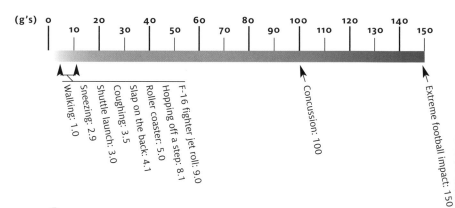

(g's) 0   10   20   30   40   50   60   70   80   90   100   110   120   130   140   150

Walking: 1.0
Sneezing: 2.9
Shuttle launch: 3.0
Coughing: 3.5
Slap on the back: 4.1
Roller coaster: 5.0
Hopping off a step: 8.1
F-16 fighter jet roll: 9.0
Concussion: 100
Extreme football impact: 150

Most people associate high g-forces with fighter pilots or astronauts. But common earthbound events can also boost g's. Few things can match the g-load of a wicked football hit.

CHAPTER 8

Golf

THE SEARCH FOR THE PERFECT GOLF SWING

by TY WENGER

IS THERE A SECRET TO ACHIEVING THE PERFECT SWING? KNOWING THE PHYSICS—AND EMPLOYING THE PROPER FUNDAMENTALS—CAN HELP UNCOVER IT.

Jack Nicklaus utilized an upright, over-the-top power fade. Arnold Palmer employed an animalistic, knee-buckling, inside-out slash. Lee Trevino aimed far to the left and sliced the ball around the course. The great Byron Nelson squatted forward like a tourist performing a hula dance.

Butch Harmon, the man who helped construct the swing that Tiger Woods used to dominate professional golf at the turn of the century, preaches the benefits of an upright "two-plane" approach. Hank Haney, the man who helped ruin and then re-build the swing that Tiger has used to dominate professional golf the past few years, evangelizes on behalf of a flat "one-plane" method.

Mike Austin, the legendary kinesiology expert credited with striking the longest drive in PGA Tour history—515 yards, *at the age of 64*—claimed that his "secret" was a forward press of the wrists, coupled with a forceful lateral shift of the hips and the casting of the club. Instructor John Novosel claims that a tempo of three beats (in the backswing) to one beat (in the downswing) is "golf's last secret," a panacea for all that ails any swing. Ben Hogan claimed to have discovered a mysterious, mythical "secret" to his swing—which, being Hogan, he never fully revealed.

Each of these men is right.

And every one of them is wrong.

Because there is, in truth, no such thing as the perfect golf swing.

Indeed, part of the reason that Hogan never fully revealed his secret (other than the fact that he was a vicious competitor who would have sooner eaten his golf tees than hand his competitors the benefit of his knowledge) was that he believed his secret (essentially, a pronation of his wrists at the top of his backswing that eliminated, for him, the dreaded pull-hook) was all but useless to anyone else. All golf swings are necessary extensions of the body employing them. And as with snowflakes and spiderwebs, no two bodies—hence no two swings—are ever exactly alike. The real secret, Hogan often said, could be found in the dirt. You've got to dig it out yourself.

At its simplest, the ultimate goal of the golf swing is merely this: deliver the club to the ball, at a high rate of speed, with the

The "Great White Shark," Greg Norman, finished first on the PGA tour twenty times before retiring in 2005.

⬥ Whether it's the inside-out slash used by Arnold Palmer (left) or the over-the-top power swing favored by Jack Nicklaus (right), great players tend to develop their own signature swing. Here, Palmer is playing at The Masters in 1965 at the Augusta National Golf Club in Augusta, Georgia; Nicklaus is shown playing in 1981.

clubface square to the target and moving, at impact, on a path directly through the ball. The point is that—to a certain degree—everything that happens prior to impact and directly after impact is, in a way, irrelevant. In truth, a golfer can swing the club from his knees (actually a useful training drill), or with a running approach (like, say, Happy Gilmore), or by eliminating the backswing altogether (as Johnny Miller experimented with back in the 1970s), so long as he can consistently and repeatedly throw the center of that clubface through the ball.

Then again, knowing the physics of the swing—and employing the proper fundamentals—makes the job all the easier. Perhaps you remember from tenth-grade physics that kinetic energy = $\frac{1}{2}$ mass X velocity^2. From the standpoint of pure physics, how much energy the club has when it collides with the ball therefore depends on only two things: the mass of the club and, far more importantly, its speed in a particular direction, or velocity. The goal of the golf swing, then, is to retain the potential energy of your club until it's converted into kinetic energy at the moment of contact with the ball. Your swing is a machine. It can be either a highly efficient one (see: Tiger Woods) or a highly inefficient one.

To build this machine, let's start from the ground up, with a strong, solid base: feet shoulder-width apart, back slightly arched, butt sticking out, knees slightly flexed, and—most often overlooked—with the weight of your body on the inside of the balls of your feet. One of the most common affronts to the physics of the golf swing occurs when a player shifts his weight too far on the backswing, allowing his center of gravity to sway to the outside of his rear foot. From there, it's nearly impossible to shift your body weight forward on the downswing. Your body acts as a dead weight, pulling backward on the swing, leading to a weak, "casted" swipe. To avoid this fate, Arnold Palmer used to practice with golf balls stuck underneath the outside of his back foot, ensuring that his weight would remain on its instep.

The grip is the next great killer of potential energy, and almost always for one reason: Most golfers grip the club too tightly. Ben Crenshaw preaches that a golfer's grip pressure should be light enough to allow the club to feel "heavy" at the top of the backswing. Sam Snead said to imagine that you're holding a live bird in your hands; you might not want him to fly away, but—unless you're some kind of sick sadist—you don't want to hurt him, either. Let your bird breathe, and you'll allow your hands to transfer, as efficiently as possible, the potential energy from your body to the clubhead. To put it another way: Nobody cracks a whip with a stiff wrist.

You can't, of course, stand there like a statue on the first tee box forever. Eventually—despite the fear of abject humiliation—you must start your backswing. And when doing so, visualize what Nick Faldo refers to as the "coiling of the spring" of the torso. While your lower body remains stable and motionless, your shoulders should turn a full 90 degrees, creating tension, or torque, between the upper and lower body. Your backswing should also be as wide as possible; aim for the sensation of reaching straight back with the club, as if trying to hand it to someone far behind you—someone who's too lazy to come and get it. The wider the arc of the swing, the greater potential clubhead velocity, as, of course, distance/time = speed.

The downswing is best thought of as a simple uncoiling of your spring, an unfolding that starts at the feet: the lower body initiates the swing, with a shift of your weight from back foot to front, initiated by the rear knee "chasing" after the front knee, causing the hips to whip around to the target, thereby rotating the torso, which pulls the shoulders around, which, in turn, drag the hands along for the ride. Allow your hands to "drop" into the swing, retaining the hinge in the wrists that you set at the top of the backswing until you release your hands at the bottom of the swing. Think of your club as the helpless last kid of a "human whip" at the roller rink—being slung along by a sum of forces far greater than any one part.

As for the follow-through? Irrelevant. In truth, a golfer could release the club from his hands the moment after impact and it would make no difference—except, of course, to your playing partners, who might not appreciate having your eight-iron embedded between their shoulder blades. Still, a full release of your arms and torso, leading to a classic pose, with your belly button pointed to the target and your hands high above your front ear? Well, that always looks nice for the cameras.

THE WOODS SWING

Golfers appear to be the most stationary of athletes, but what separates Tiger Woods, the dominant golfer of modern times, from the rest of the pack is his speed.

No, we're not talking about how quickly he gets from one hole to another. The key to Tiger Woods's success is the tremendous speed of his swing, with recorded clubhead speeds at upwards of 130 mph, and ball speeds that approach 200 mph off his driver. And

what's fascinating about Tiger is that he's now been able to achieve those speeds with three different swings—and two totally different body types.

When he first burst onto the golf scene in 1996, Tiger was a whip-thin prodigy (6-foot-1 and 155 pounds) who generated his enormous distances through both an outrageously supple and forceful unwinding of his torso and a fairly radical "de-lofting" of his clubs at impact. At the time, Tiger would flatten his left wrist at impact, turning his five-iron, in essence, into a four-iron, and also reducing the spin on the ball, resulting in laser-like, flat-trajectory swings and balls that flew inconceivable distances (much farther than he hits it now). The problem: As an inevitable result of this, he had little idea where, or how far, his ball would fly.

After decimating the field in the 1997 Masters with this swing (the result of what Tiger would call a perfect week of rhythm and timing in his swing), he set out to rebuild it with the aid of Butch Harmon—shortening it, tightening it, making it more upright, and, most importantly, trying to eliminate his longtime tendency to get the club "stuck" behind him, a swing flaw that resulted in wild misses to the right of the fairway. This rebuilt swing produced the run of golf from 1999 to 2003 that was as dominant as any in the history of the game.

Unfortunately, it was unsustainable. The golf swing is a violent act, and Tiger's had begun to produce debilitating wear on his left knee. One result of his upright swing was that he would often hyperextend his left knee at impact, stressing several of the tendons. Forced to change after undergoing a second surgery on the knee in 2003, he sought the counsel of Hank Haney, who advocates a swing theory in almost diametric opposition to what Harmon had been teaching Tiger. Haney believes in a flat one-plane swing, which eliminates—in theory—much of the extraneous body action that was plaguing Woods. After a

year or two of, essentially, reteaching himself to swing the club, Tiger emerged as a dominant force again, winning five of twelve majors from 2004 to 2007, with more than twenty worldwide wins. He still generates the same amazing swing speeds, but he now does so with a flatter plane that puts less strain on his front knee, and Tiger is also better suited to accommodate the physics of the thicker, more muscular body type of a man approaching middle age. In other words, the tour should beware: Tiger has rebuilt himself for the long haul.

DRIVERS AT SPEED

Clubhead speed for the average golfer with an iron is more than 80 mph when it hits the ball. With a driver, it nears 100 mph (with a ceiling of 125–130 mph for the longest-hitting pros). The club maintains contact with the ball for only one millisecond and exerts a

force of 660 pounds. Initial ball speed off a driver is, for most pros, about 150 mph—upwards of 180 mph for such kinesiological freaks as Tiger Woods and John Daly.

NEW BALLS FALL SHORT
by DAVID GOULD

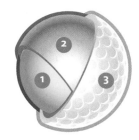

Augusta National Golf Club is fond of tradition, but renovating its golf course to accommodate increasingly longer drives is a practice the club has wearied of. The course has seen a 6.6 percent yardage increase over seven years (7,445 yards for the 2006 Masters Tournament compared to 6,985 in 1999)—the equivalent of one hole. That's led the influential club to join course architects and others in a push for new equipment regulations.

The U.S. Golf Association is listening and, in a first for the sports world, equipment manufacturers are being asked to make their products worse. Golf-ball makers have been told to submit prototypes that fly 15 to 25 yards shorter than current balls when driven at 120 mph. Reducing yardage will invariably mean rolling back technological advances that, over the past decade, have made the modern golf ball do its job so well. Too well, in fact.

1 **Advance:** Polybutadiene-based core boosts velocity for drives.
Rollback: "Unlink" the molecular structure for less efficient energy transfer.

2 **Advance:** Mantle increases acceleration and regulates spin.
Rollback: Soften the mantle so the ball regains its round shape less quickly.

3 **Advance:** Refined dimple shapes and geometry reduce drag.
Rollback: Revert to prior dimple configurations, increasing drag.

Longer drives have led Augusta to add 85 yards to the seventh hole.

Hockey

SKATE FASTER

by LAURA STAMM

HOCKEY IS ALL ABOUT SPEED. TO ACHIEVE IT, ONE MUST APPLY THE PRINCIPLES OF FORCE APPLICATION EXPLOSIVELY AND WITH PRECISE TIMING (POWER). WHILE RAPID LEG MOTION IS IMPORTANT, SO IS THE CORRECT AND POWERFUL USE OF THE BLADE EDGES, LEGS, AND BODY WEIGHT. TOO MANY PLAYERS ARE TAUGHT TO MOVE THEIR FEET FAST REGARDLESS OF WHETHER OR NOT THEY ARE FOLLOWING THE PRINCIPLES OF FORCE APPLICATION. THESE PLAYERS MOVE AS IF ON A TREADMILL, WORKING HARD BUT GOING NOWHERE.

Eastern Conference competitor Miroslav Satan, No. 81 of the Buffalo Sabres, competes in the Fastest Skater event during the 53rd NHL All-Star Weekend on February 1, 2003, in Sunrise, Florida. The Western Conference won 15–9.

I created the C-cut exercise in 1971, and it remains one of my signature drills to this day. I named the push a C-cut because in executing the push, the skate scribes a cut in the ice that is similar to the letter "C" or a semicircular arc. The C-cut push is used for both forward and backward skating moves. This exercise focuses on the first third of the push for the forward stride that involves the heel (the midsole and the toe constitute the other parts). When done properly, the drill helps you develop a powerful push that generates speed.

ADVANTAGES OF THE C-CUT

In executing the forward C-cut, first the pushing leg moves to the back, then it curves out to extend sideways, moves forward, and completes the C by curving back to its starting position beneath the midline of the body. The C-cut exercise incorporates important skating and training fundamentals including:

> using the inside edges to cut powerfully into the ice when pushing

> thrusting first to the back and then to the side rather than directly back

> training the body to experience a fully extended, straightened free leg and a maximum-effort thrust, rather than a partially extended, weaker push

> training the gliding and pushing legs to work independently (while the glide is straightforward on a well-bent knee, the push is semicircular and the leg extends fully at the completion of the push)

> using the heel to begin each push of the forward stride (The toe of the blade is not used in the C-cut push; you push only with the back of the blade.)

The forward C-cut forms an upside-down letter C. In other words, the push begins at the bottom of the C and ends at the top of the C. The backward C-cut is exactly the reverse. The forward C-cut is skated with both skates on the ice at all times. Here's the twelve-step program designed to rid you of slowness on the ice. The left leg is the initial pushing leg.

1. Glide forward on the flats of both skates, feet directly under your body. Keep your back straight.

2. Prepare to push with the left leg while gliding straight ahead on the flat of the right skate.

3. Keep your weight on the back half of the thrusting (left) skate.

4. Bend your knees and dig the inside edge of the left skate into the ice so the skate and knee form a 45-degree angle to the ice. Concentrate your body weight over the edge.

5. Pivot the left foot outward with toe facing out to the side so that your skates approximate a right angle. Heels will be together and toes will be apart. You are now prepared to execute a C-cut push.

6. Cut the letter C into the ice with the left skate by pushing to the back, then outward until the pushing leg is fully extended out to the side.

7. At the mid-point of the C-cut thrust, transfer your weight onto the right skate, which is gliding straight ahead on the flat of the blade.

8. Thrust powerfully and to full extension. Keep the thrusting skate on the ice after the thrust is completed. The knee of the gliding leg remains well bent even when the thrusting leg is fully extended.

9. After the leg reaches its full extension, re-pivot the left skate. The left toe should now face inward (pigeon-toed) toward the gliding skate. This step is necessary in order to return the skate to its starting

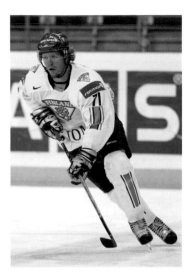

Tomi Kallio, No. 71 of Finland, executes the C-cut during warm-ups before the 2006 International Ice Hockey Federation World Championship qualifying game between Canada and Finland at Riga Arena in Riga, Latvia.

position under your body. During the return, the skate no longer cuts into the ice. It glides back into the center under the body.

10. Move the left leg forward and then inward to its starting position centered underneath your body.

11. After the return, your feet should be side-by-side and centered under your body.

12. After returning, the left skate becomes the new gliding skate. To push again, place your weight on the inside edge of the right skate and cut a reverse and upside-down letter C with your right leg. Pivot the right skate, toe outward, and push front to back, then out to the side in a full extension. Then re-pivot the right skate (pigeon-toed) and bring it forward and then inward to its starting position centered under your body weight.

Remember: the push is a C-cut, not a silent C. The skate must cut into the ice. You should hear it. The sound indicates that your weight is over the pushing skate with the inside edge gripping the ice strongly.

The C-cut differs from the forward stride motion in that while the C-cut ends on your heel, the forward stride ends on your toe. Nevertheless, C-cut drills will improve your forward glide and help you develop the ability to generate more power off the initial push, and that will translate into faster skating.

FOR GOALIES, IT'S THE EYES THAT MATTER

by FRANK VIZARD

A FAST GLOVE AND A QUICK STICK MAY MATTER LESS TO HOCKEY GOALIES THAN WHERE THEY FOCUS THEIR EYES IN THE MOMENTS BEFORE AN OPPOSING PLAYER TAKES A SHOT ON GOAL.

While it may sound obvious, having your eyes focused on the puck and the shooter's stick in the second before the shot means the goalie is more likely to make the save, according to researchers at the University of Calgary.

Researchers Derek Panchuk and Professor Joan Vickers call this the Quiet Eye phenomenon, noting that novice goaltenders tend to let their gaze wander while elite goaltenders remain focused on the puck and shooter's stick. Vickers describes the Quiet Eye phenomenon as the critical moment when the eyes must receive and the brain must process the last piece of visual information before performing a critical movement. Using wireless headgear, the researchers were able to track a goalie's eye, body, and object movement to within 16.67 milliseconds. How far away the shot was didn't seem to matter in terms of a goalie's ability to make the save, as long as the puck was in view a second before the shot.

The study measured the eye movement of college-level goalies facing accomplished shooters one-on-one in a non-game situation. The goalies stopped the puck about 75 percent of the time under these conditions. In games, elite hockey goalies average about a 90 percent save rate, although the quality of the shots taken varies considerably.

SIX DEGREES OF SEPARATION

A goalie concentrating on the game.

22 DEGREES F. Temperature of ice in rink preferred by figure skaters who like "soft" ice for better landings on jumps.

16 DEGREES F. Temperature preferred by hockey players who like a "fast" ice that allows for more speed.

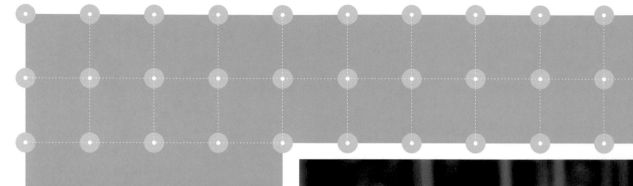

HOW BIG IS
YOUR STICK?

by FRANK VIZARD

FOR MANY PLAYERS,
THE SIZE OF THE
CURVE IN THE BLADE
MAY MEAN THE
DIFFERENCE BETWEEN
AN ORDINARY
CAREER AND A
STELLAR ONE.

When hockey legend Brett Hull, who scored 943 goals with the St. Louis Blues and other teams, confessed to *Sports Illustrated* magazine that he used an illegal stick for most of his career, the revelation created a only minor tempest. Why? Unlike a corked bat in baseball, for example, the benefit of an illegal stick with a more pronounced curve on the blade is harder to definitely gauge in hockey.

In 2006, the National Hockey League changed its rule on how much curve in a blade is allowed, upping the limit to three-quarters of an inch from a half-inch. Scorers like Alex Ovechkin of the Washington Clippers, who was just coming off a 52-goal season, salivated in anticipation of the effect a 50 percent increase in the curvature of the blade would have on their goal production. By the end of the 2006–7 season, the effect was negligible. Ovechkin actually finished with 46 goals, and there was no noticeable uptick in scoring throughout the league.

Cynics might suggest that this only means most players were already using illegal sticks, perhaps since the three-quarter-inch blade was legal at the international and Olympic levels. Hockey players are notoriously attached to their sticks. The rush to the stick rack at the ten-minute mark of many games seemed to suggest that players were switching from legal to illegal sticks before an opposing coach could invoke the illegal-stick rule, if the score was close and the switch might affect the outcome of the contest. And should a player be caught with an illegal stick, the rule violation is considered a minor penalty and the fine is $200. Brett calls the regulation a "stupid rule" put it in place to protect goalies when they weren't very well padded and lacked helmets.

So what advantage can a longer curve on the blade of a stick provide? According to Alain Heche, a physicist at Moncton University and author of *The Physics of Hockey*, a longer curve should not add to the velocity of a shot puck, as speed is more of a by-product of the force with which the puck is hit. What a longer curve does provide is more consistency, since the puck always leaves the stick at the same place. The longer curve also gives a player more control of the puck, making it both easier to carry the puck around defenders and to grab the puck with the tip of the

Right wing Brett Hull, No. 16 of the Phoenix Coyotes, skates against the Mighty Ducks of Anaheim during their preseason game at Arrowhead Pond in Anaheim, California, in September 2005.

blade and shoot upward in one motion. A longer curve also puts more spin on the puck, which gives the puck more stability, making it that much more likely that the puck will go where a player is aiming. The reason for the curvature rule, notes Heche, is probably to limit puck control. In any event, any added benefit would be difficult to measure or even detect, he adds.

For many players, the size of the curve in the blade may mean the difference between an ordinary career and a stellar one. Brett Hull said he couldn't shoot without the curve on his stick. The question now is whether blades longer than three-quarters of an inch will appear, perhaps even approaching the banana-sized proportions used by Brett's father, Hall-of-Famer Bobby Hull. So keep an eye on the stick rack as the game winds down, when some players might switch to their illegal sticks. The team that risks playing with the most illegal sticks could have a deciding advantage.

PUCK SCIENCE

MATERIAL: Vulcanized rubber.

COLOR: Black.

SIZE: three inches in diameter, one inch thick.

WEIGHT: 5.5 to 5.6 ounces.

EDGE: Series of grooves or bumps so a taped hockey stick has something to grip on contact.

STORAGE: In freezers during a game to reduce bounce.

ORIGIN OF NAME: Unknown, but some suggest the name comes from the character of the same name in Shakespeare's *A Midsummer Night's Dream* as both move quickly and often in unexpected directions.

DATE OF INVENTION: The first puck was allegedly made around 1875 when Boston University students cut a rubber ball in half for use in a game.

BEST TV MOMENT: The 1995–96 NHL season when the Fox television network embedded a computer chip and cut twenty pinholes in the puck so that sensors could track it around the ice and viewers could find it more easily. At high speeds, the pucks developed a halo effect. Players complained that the puck didn't perform as well as the original. The idea was dropped.

DISTANCE A PUCK WILL TRAVEL ON ICE: If unimpeded by the rink, a puck shot at a speed of 100 mph—typical for a slap shot—would travel almost 1.2 miles (1.9 km) in 2 minutes 15 seconds, according to Professor Alain Heche of Moncton University in Canada.

WHY GRETZKY IS THE GREATEST

In a 1997 magazine interview, former St. Louis Blues goalie Mike Liut boiled the skill set of Wayne Gretzky, perhaps the greatest hockey player ever, down to a single question: "What don't I see that Wayne's seeing right now?"

By his own admission, Gretzky, who played most famously with the Edmonton Oilers as well as several other teams during the 1980s and 1990s, was not the strongest or fastest or most agile player on the ice even though he was named MVP of the National Hockey League nine times. What Gretzky did have was an ability that amounted to being able to see into the future and visualize what was going to happen in the next few seconds. In an article appearing in *Wired* magazine, scientists working for the U.S. Olympic team and the Australian Institute of Sport concluded that skills like Gretzky's come from an innate ability to intuitively translate physical cues dropped by opponents that are not apparent to most other athletes. Scientists are at work figuring out how this skill can be taught, but this type of perceptual training is still in its infancy. On the other hand, Gretzky may have just been following his father's advice, given to him when he was a youngster: "Skate to where the puck is going to be, not where it has been."

All-Star Wayne Gretzky was said to have a magic touch with the puck, an accolade that stemmed from his great vision and mobility on the ice.

CHAPTER 10

Running

MARATHON RUNNING

by DR. JOE VIGIL

DR. JOE VIGIL IS A LEGEND IN THE WORLD OF MARATHON RUNNING AND HAS BEEN LAUDED AS A "COACH SCIENTIST" FOR HIS ABILITY TO COMBINE SCIENCE AND ATHLETIC TRAINING DURING HIS 30-YEAR CAREER. VIGIL COACHED DEENA KASTOR TO A MARATHON BRONZE MEDAL AT THE 2004 OLYMPIC GAMES IN ATHENS, GREECE, CAPPING AN OLYMPIC TEAM ASSOCIATION DATING TO 1968. HERE, VIGIL, WHO BELIEVES DISTANCE RUNNING IS ENJOYING A RENAISSANCE, BREAKS DOWN A MARATHON.

Deena Kastor of the United States runs through the tape to win the women's 26th London Marathon on the Mall in front of Buckingham Palace on April 23, 2006. Kastor's time was 2:19:36.

PRIOR TO THE START

I pay attention to what a runner drinks 30 minutes before the start. You want to make sure the runner has enough liquids. I pre-determine how many ounces a runner should drink based on his or her size. We mix two powders, Accelerate and Endurox, with liquid. The mixture is four parts carbohydrate and one part protein. I make sure a runner is well hydrated and well fueled. If the race is early in the morning, a runner might eat a piece of toast or a bagel with jelly two or three hours before the marathon. You don't run the marathon on what you eat that day. You run on the fuel reserves you have built up from the previous days.

AT THE STARTING LINE

When a runner goes to the starting line, he or she already knows the course and the competition. Runners know what pace they are going to have to maintain. Olympic medalist Deena Kastor, for example, has a pre-determined pace that she is going to maintain. She knows how she feels at that pace because she has done it so many times in training. We determine that several different ways. I like to put her on a treadmill and determine her velocity at a respiratory quotient (RQ) of .94. That is the point at which she is burning pure fat more or less. This number can vary a hundredth of a percent from day to day because your metabolism varies from day to day as well. I've used .94 because it is a pretty good figure that you can rely on. In Deena's case, her velocity was 5 minutes 20 seconds per mile burning pure fat. That's what marathoners try to do. They try to utilize the energy derived from fat for the majority of the marathon. Everyone is different, though, in that runners will reach their .94 RQ at a different velocity. With Deena, her RQ velocity might go up or down a second on any given day depending upon her metabolism and the enzymes she has available. That's why you want to establish some constancy in the athlete in his or her eating and resting habits, so that it is about the same all the time. You have to live the lifestyle. The more variables you can control, the more predictable the result, just like any scientific experiment.

Mebrahtom Keflezighi of the United States enters the stadium before finishing second to win the Silver Medal in the men's marathon on August 29, 2004, during the 2004 Summer Olympic Games at Panathinaiko Stadium in Athens, Greece.

The first couple of miles, you have a great number of runners to contend with and there is a lot of nervous energy at play. You're trying to get away from the starting point to avoid injury and to prevent anyone from running into you. So sometimes you have to run a little faster than you would like that first mile to make space between you and the people behind you. If you're going to run in the lead group, you want to position yourself to be in contact with them.

Once you have good position, you settle down to your race pace. But here again, you're not always able to maintain a race pace if you have undulating terrain or if you have to run uphill or if the roar of the crowd is such that it motivates you—like the crowd coming off the 59th Street Bridge onto First Avenue in the New York Marathon. All runners experience a high when they hear people cheering. They can run a mile that is fifteen or twenty seconds faster than their race pace. You have to be careful. A marathon runner must always have emotional control over his or her pace. You can't be suckered into running someone else's race. That's why marathon runners should know themselves and the sensation of effort they are feeling at a particular pace. Once we've tested people and tell them what their relative pace might be, that's where we do the bulk of the training. Not all of it, because we challenge different energy systems. But since the marathon is a highly aerobic event, we spend 98 percent of our time within the aerobic range. If they do a hard aerobic run at marathon pace for 20 to 25 miles, the next day we'll schedule a low-intensity recovery run.

As the race progresses, we encounter other stresses. Is the wind blowing? Is it hot or humid? Is it raining or snowing? We then adjust our pace accordingly. When Deena ran the Olympic marathon in Athens, for example, it was 100 degrees at 6 p.m. and the newly laid asphalt was 120 degrees. When the men ran the marathon a week later, it was 85 degrees. The temperature determined how fast you could go because you had to endure the heat and the humidity for a longer period of time, and it takes more of an effort. Heat and humidity are the biggest stressors in the marathon. Deena started out relatively slowly. Because I had studied the past five Olympic marathons and the past six national championships, we knew what kind of time Deena had to run in order to medal.

Marathon runners are not as strong as sprinters. They don't have the muscle mass to produce the power to drive. The greater the force of the implant on the ground or track, the more driving force you get from the ground, especially on all-weather tracks that are so resilient they give energy back.

In a marathon, size works against you. Oxygen consumption is per kilogram of body weight. The bigger you are, the more calories you're going to burn. Efficient oxygen use, by the way, is very important. By slowly increasing her training runs to 100 to 110 miles per week, Deena gradually increased her VO2 MAX number—the amount of oxygen your body can use in one minute per kilogram of body weight—from 70.2 milliliters to 81.3 milliliters, one of the highest figures ever recorded for an American female athlete.

When you consider a marathon lasts two hours plus, any strength marathoners can develop, any fluidity in their mechanics that will enhance their striding pattern so that they can cover more ground per stride, is what they should shoot for. If you ran a 28-minute, 10,000-meter race and you improved your stride length two-thousandths of an inch per stride—that's derived from strength and power—you can lower that 10,000-meter time to 26 minutes flat. The most efficient running is evenly paced running. But not everyone can run an even pace. You have to know your body well. After nine years of coaching Deena, I would say that she is now finally in tune with her body in terms of marathon running. It's not an overnight phenomenon.

RUNNING THE MIDDLE MILES

Every runner knows what time he or she is supposed to hit at each mile or kilometer marker. If you're hitting these markers and you're running an even pace but find yourself in 100th place, you can't worry about it because you're running to your capacity. If you're leading the field, it tends to have a synergistic effect in that you start thinking you're really good and you run a little faster. If you're struggling to maintain your pace and people are ahead of you, you start thinking negative thoughts and that works against you. The mind is very powerful, and your mental state throughout the race is a determining factor in how successful you're going to be.

Because Deena looked so good when she won a bronze in Athens, people asked why she didn't run faster sooner. It's because she had an eight-mile incline to contemplate in addition to the heat and the humidity. Many women dropped out of the race, including world-record holder Paula Radcliffe at the 30K mark. If Deena had come out fast, she might have encountered the same difficulty. Instead, she had a negative split—meaning she ran the second half of the race faster than the first. She ran the last five kilometers in 16:09, partly because it was downhill. It also helped that I had found a course in California just like the one in Athens, and she ran it seven times at altitude before we went to Athens. I

Aerial view of New York City Marathon runners crossing the Verrazano-Narrows Bridge near the start of the race on November 3, 1996.

believe in the three A's: attitude, aptitude, and altitude. If you don't train at altitude, you're not going to compete with the best in the world. Over the past 20 years, people who live at altitude or who train at altitude have won 95 percent of the medals. By living and training at altitude, athletes can increase their red blood cell mass, which in turn enhances the athlete's oxygen-carrying capability.

HITTING THE WALL

The wall is the point at which you have depleted your level of carbohydrates. If you run faster than your RQ pace for an extended period of time, you will start using glycogen instead of fat. Deena's RQ velocity was 5:20, and that's the point where she is burning pure fat. You use fat as your source of energy and save your carbohydrates for the end. If you don't properly train, you'll race too fast and you won't be running aerobically, so you'll use up your carbohydrates or glucose. Whenever you use up your glucose, you hit the wall. You train to push the wall somewhere past the finish line. That's why pace is important in the marathon. If you know yourself, you'll maintain that pace at which you're burning fat. In your training, you're trying to develop the fastest velocity possible at which you're burning fat.

You can't hit the wall early during the race. You have about 410 grams of carbohydrates or glucose in your body. Each gram yields 4 calories of energy, so your glucose concentration will contribute 1,600 calories toward the marathon effort. Each gram of fat in your body contributes 9 calories toward the marathon effort. So it only stands to reason you would use the energy from fat because you have twice the amount of energy available (nine grams per calorie). And your stored fats are available in sufficient quantities that you could run many marathons provided you ran slowly enough. You need to save the glucose for the end of the race.

The problem, however, is marathon runners tend to be lean. Elite woman marathoners have a body fat of between 10 and 12 percent, while elite men are in the range of 4 to 8 percent. It's difficult to add body fat when you're training hard. But there is also a thing we call "critical fat," which is the percentage of fat that you have to maintain in order for normal metabolism, hormone and enzyme production, to take place. The critical point for women is 9 percent body fat and for men it is 3 percent. So you never want to go below that or you have to cut back on training. Ideally, a woman should stay above 10 percent and a man above 4 percent.

You can run a marathon on less than one pound of fat. One pound of fat yields 3,500 calories, and it normally takes about 2,700 to 2,800 calories for a man to run a marathon and 2,400 calories for a woman. So everyone has the energy to do it, but the pace is the regulator of how that energy is going to be used. You have to have emotional control during the race or you won't have the energy to finish it. You have to know a little something about your body and what it is capable of. That's the hard part with coaching.

THE LAST FEW MILES

The race doesn't really begin until the last five or six miles. What happens now is that runners start surging, testing one another. One runner will surge to see who will stay with him or her. At a given point, they will break into a fast mile of about 4:30. With a surge you are trying to upset a competitor's pace, but you run the risk of ruining your own. So you practice surging, asking runners to run faster than race pace the last two or three miles of a tempo run. But at this point in the competition, a lot of runners will be running beyond their capacity. Surges will narrow the field because some runners are forced to dip into their carbohydrate bank for additional energy.

If there are runners bunched together with 400 meters to go, then the marathon becomes a sprint. This is where the carbohydrates or glucose is expended. This is where runners tap into different energy sources called the alactate and lactate systems to sprint the last few yards if need be. At this point, it is a question of who can hang on to win. The biggest excitement for me is that I know what it takes to achieve those world-class times. I've developed a lot of respect for those athletes who can stick to a regimen and produce those results.

TALKING SHOE

What's the future of the running shoe? How about a shoe that talks to you? A running shoe from Nike is able to send data wirelessly to Apple's portable iPod music player, allowing a runner to monitor his performance while listening to downloaded coaching advice. Runners also will be able to upload their personal stats onto a Nike website and compare them with others. Where Nike leads, others are sure to follow.

The Nike + iPod Sport Kit is basically a small oval pod that fits under the liner of the running shoe. It looks much like a SIM card used in a cellphone, and it transmits a variety of data such as time and distance to a receiver that connects to your iPod. Apple also offers special workout music mixes that can be downloaded to the iPod so that inspirational music can get you past the next milestone.

CHIPS FOR SHOES

The future of running shoes may have already arrived in the form of a running shoe that uses a computer to adjust itself during the

course of the run. The Adidas_1 Intelligence Level 1.1 is equipped with a small sensor and a magnet that tells a tiny computer embedded in the shoe when the cushioning level is too soft or too firm. The sensor sits just below the runner's heel, and the magnet is placed at the bottom of the midsole. The system gauges the compression on impact and deduces the amount of cushioning being employed. About 1,000 readings per second are relayed to the

computer located under the arch of the shoe. By comparing the incoming data against a preset model, the shoe can determine if the cushioning is too soft or too hard. The microprocessor then commands a motor-driven cable to either tighten or loosen a screw accordingly. The entire system runs off a small battery—so the next time you see a runner adjusting his shoe, he may not be tying his shoelaces but replacing a battery.

PICK THE RIGHT SHOE

Picking the right running shoe depends upon the type of foot you have. Foot types can basically be lumped into three categories: normal, flat, and arched. Match the right shoe to the right foot type and you'll avoid a lot of pain.

So which type of foot do you have? Find out by wetting a pair of brown bags and then standing on them in your bare feet. The resulting imprint will tell you a lot.

If the heel and the ball of the footprint are connected and there is a slight indentation where the arch is, then you have normal feet. When running, a normal foot generally lands on the outside of the heel with a slight inward roll on each stride. All the foot needs is a little stabilization, so look for a shoe with a firm sole and a slight curve on the bottom.

Flat feet that have little or no arch tend to roll too far inward. This puts too much of the body's weight on the inner sole and, in time, may lead to pain in the ankles and hips. A shoe that compensates for this pronation should have a very stiff midsole to keep the foot from rolling too far inward.

By contrast, feet with high arches require a shoe flexible enough to let the foot roll inward more. Otherwise, high arches can cause feet to roll over on their edges. A well-cushioned, slightly curved running shoe usually corrects the problem.

Like a car that needs to change its tires after a number of miles, you should expect to change running shoes every 300 to 500 miles. If you feel a twinge in your legs where there was none before, or fatigue in your hips and knees, it may be an early sign that your running shoe needs replacement.

CHAPTER 11

Skiing

SPEED SKIING

by CHARLES
PLUEDDEMAN

SPEED SKIING, THE PURSUIT OF PEAK VELOCITY, IS THE MOST INTENSE AND THRILLING OF ALL THE SKIING DISCIPLINES. WIND TEARS AT YOUR BODY AND THE SKIS FLOP AS YOU FIGHT TO HOLD A TUCK POSITION. AS YOU HURTLE DOWN THE COURSE, PASSING THROUGH TIMING LIGHTS, YOUR BODY PUNCHES A HOLE IN THE ATMOSPHERE THAT RIPS THE AIR WITH A JET-ENGINE ROAR. SLOWING DOWN IN THE BRAKING AREA, YOU GLANCE AT THE SCOREBOARD TO SEE YOUR SPEED CLOCKED IN EXCESS OF 140 MPH. ANY FASTER AND YOU'D NEED A PARACHUTE.

Sanna Tidstrand of Sweden competes on her way to capturing the women's Gold Medal at the FIS Speed Skiing World Championships in Verbier, Switzerland, in April 2007.

THE HISTORY OF SPEED SKIING

The origin of speed skiing dates to 1898, when a Californian, Tommy Todd, allegedly zipped to 87 mph (about 139 kph). However, the first official record was set in 1932, when Italian skier Leo Gasperi was clocked at 89 mph (about 142 kph) by the International Ski Federation / Fédération Internationale de Ski (FIS) in St. Moritz, Switzerland. By the 1960s, speed skiing was a professional sport sanctioned by the FIS. It was also accorded the status of a demonstration sport in the 1992 Winter Olympics in Albertville, France.

SPECIALIZED EQUIPMENT

The basic goal of speed skiing is to harness gravity and defeat friction. To this end, the equipment is highly specialized. The skis are about 240 centimeters long, compared to 225 centimeters for a downhill racing ski and 200 centimeters for a recreational ski. In addition, the skis are 10 centimeters wide and made of wood and steel, which contributes to their hefty 25-pound weight.

The extra width helps the skis run flat on the snow and spread out the skier's weight over the largest possible area to reduce friction. To keep the tips on the snow at speeds over 100 mph, the skis are rigid, heavily damped, and shaped to cut a low profile for minimal wind resistance.

While speed skiers use widely available high-performance bindings and boots, they typically fit the bindings with a stiff racing spring and modify the boot cuffs to provide a sharp forward lean in the lower leg, which allows the racer to bend low in the tuck position.

To help air pass smoothly over their bodies, speed skiers squeeze into skintight suits. The suit's material is typically a stretch fabric that may be coated with polyurethane, for example, to give it density to resist the formation of slipstream bubbles in low-pressure zones along the racer's body. Each suit is custom-cut to fit the racer's body.

To smooth the airflow around the lower legs, a wedge-shaped fairing made of dense foam fits inside the suit behind each calf from the knee to the boot top. Interestingly, airflow concerns also play a part in glove design. Speed skiers use their hands as the leading edge to break the wind and to act as a controlling rudder. The gloves, also made of a stretch material, have special cuffs that allow the air to flow smoothly over the wrists.

Speed skiers use poles to push off at the starting point and to act as a framework for bracing their arms next to their bodies. The poles are custom-bent to wrap around a skier's torso. Cones fitted to the end of each grip also help to streamline air.

According to U.S. speed skier Jeff Hamilton, the speed skier's helmet is his most essential piece of equipment. Hamilton should know. In 1995, he was ranked the fastest skier in the world, with a mark of 242 kph (150.4 mph) set in Vars, France.

"Each helmet is custom-made to fit the racer's body size and tuck position," explains Hamilton. "It directs wind from the top of the head in a straight line down the back. A slight change in the shape of the helmet can cause a one-mile-per-hour or more difference in top speed."

Hamilton's helmet was molded from a combination of Kevlar and fiberglass. Some helmets are designed with a fin along the top to increase stability and to allow the racer to steer by moving his head.

Another essential element is the preparation of the ski bases. Hamilton tuned his skis to fit conditions by using a stone grinder to create varied structural patterns and then applied one of several types of wax. There are only about ten speed-skiing courses in the world capable of hosting a World Cup–level event. Each course must be able to safely produce speeds of at least 170 kph (about 106 mph).

THE RACING COURSE

The racer's speed potential is dictated by the location of the starting point, which is typically 300 to 400 meters (984–1,312 feet) above the first timing light. Race officials determine the starting point after calculating snow and weather conditions, the steepness of the hill, and the ability of the athletes entered in the race. In an effort to promote safety, the FIS has mandated that a starting point must be chosen that will not produce a speed above

⚫ Two views of the speed skier's tuck. Boots are modified to provide a sharp forward lean. The head is lower than the butt so that airflow on the back produces downward pressure. Note the aerodynamic contours of the helmet.

228 kph (about 142 mph). The rule is intended to encourage athletes to compete for the fastest speed at each event, rather than just gunning for a new record. When a record is set, it is a true accomplishment.

Skiers study the course before each run and pick the smoothest path to the speed trap: two sets of timing lights set 100 meters (about 328 feet) apart. To start, the skier simply stands perpendicular to the fall line of the hill, picks his line, and then jumps to face downhill. From there, gravity and technique take over.

Since skiers reach top speed in less than 400 meters (1,312 feet), initial acceleration is critical. Ski tuning plays an important role here, as does the technique of keeping flat on the snow and maintaining an optimal tuck position: head low and butt high to create downward pressure. Initially, Hamilton holds his hands positioned in front of his helmet, but as he builds speed he gradually extends his arms out about eight inches in front of his body.

In less than fifteen seconds, acceleration goes from zero to more than 225 kph (140 mph). The entire run takes just twenty seconds, but it is a very intense twenty seconds with little margin for error.

A red line in the snow signals the end of the speed trap, and the skier begins the process of slowing down—the most dangerous part of the run. On slower courses, where speeds don't go much above 161 kph (100 mph), skiers can just stand up and use the wind as a brake. But at 225 kph (140 mph), you must slowly untuck to dirty the aerodynamics. Below 161 kph (100 mph), you can carve very wide turns to burn off speed.

For each round in a multi-day event, the starting point is moved higher up the hill. There are four to six rounds in a typical meet, and the fastest skier in the final round is declared the winner.

Defying the best efforts of the FIS, speed skiers continue to bump the world speed record upward at sanctioned meets. Is there a limit to speed on the snow?

For years, many skiers considered 250 kph (155.343 mph) a "mythical border,"—but in 2002 it was passed by Philippe Goitschel at Les Arcs, France, with a speed of 250.70 kph (155.778 mph). That record has since been broken by Simone Origone, who clocked in at 252.4 kph (156.834 mph) at Les Arcs in 2006.

SKI JUMPING: IN-FLIGHT ADJUSTMENTS

by ALEX HUTCHINSON

IT'S WELL ESTABLISHED THAT A SKI JUMPER'S BODY AND SKIS WORK LIKE AN AIRPLANE WING.

They direct the onrushing wind downward, forcing the air rushing over the top of the body and skis to flow faster than the air below. In a demonstration of Bernoulli's principle, this creates lower pressure on the topside of the skier than below him, pulling him upward. But ski jumpers aren't just like airplane wings—they're like airplane wings with precise controls. Austrian researchers Bernhard Schmölzer and Wolfram Müller studied competitors at the 2002 Olympics, where the jumping was held in Park City, Utah, at an unusually high altitude of more than 6,500 feet. Top jumpers compensated for the decreased lift (and drag) of the thin air by adjusting the angle between their bodies and skis to an average of 16.1 degrees, greater than the 11.7 degrees seen at lower elevations. The 2006 Olympic ski-jumping events were held at 5,000 feet in the Italian town of Pragelato.

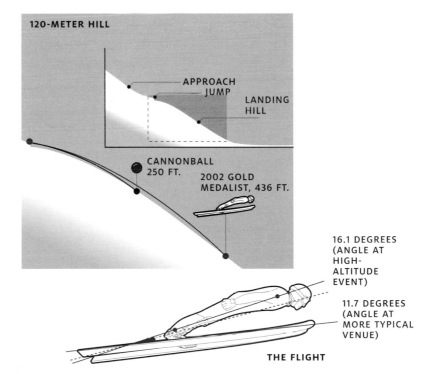

120-METER HILL

APPROACH
JUMP

LANDING
HILL

CANNONBALL
250 FT.

2002 GOLD
MEDALIST, 436 FT.

16.1 DEGREES
(ANGLE AT
HIGH-
ALTITUDE
EVENT)

11.7 DEGREES
(ANGLE AT
MORE TYPICAL
VENUE)

THE FLIGHT

▶ In 2002, airfoil-like ski-jumping champion Simon Ammann flew 186 feet farther than if—like a cannonball—he'd experienced no lift.

◀ Ski jumpers such as champion Simon Ammann can widen the angle between their bodies and skis to gain lift.

SNOWBOARDING'S TWISTING FORCES

by ALEX HUTCHINSON

Olympic snowboarder Danny Kass is brilliant at improvising during his halfpipe runs, says U.S. Olympic coach Mike Jankowski. But some things are set the instant he launches from the lip of the eighteen-foot-high pipe. The path his center of mass will take—how high he soars and where he lands—is determined by his approach. And the angular momentum for the flips and rotations he does fifteen feet off the deck must be generated before he leaves the snow. Top riders can spin through 1440 degrees (four rotations), but more in the spirit of the sport are the back-to-back inverted 1080s that Kass pioneered—which use every trick in Isaac Newton's playbook.

Olympic medalist Danny Kass rules the halfpipe. During this classic move—a cork frontside 720—he does a tail grab and inverts while spinning through 720 degrees. He sets up all of the rotational forces for the trick while he's still on terra froza.

Soccer

BEND IT LIKE BECKHAM

by FRANK VIZARD

IF YOU'RE EVEN REMOTELY FAMILIAR WITH SOCCER, THEN YOU KNOW THAT THE PHRASE "BEND IT LIKE BECKHAM" HAS ENTERED THE SPORTS LEXICON AND EVEN APPEARED AS THE TITLE OF A POPULAR BRITISH FILM IN 2002. BECKHAM, OF COURSE, IS DAVID BECKHAM, THE FORMER SUPERSTAR OF ENGLISH SOCCER. BUT WHAT'S THIS "BEND IT" BUSINESS ALL ABOUT?

British soccer legend David Beckham.

THE INFAMOUS SHOT

It's October 6, 2001. England is playing Greece. A qualifying berth in the World Cup is on the line. In the waning seconds of the game, the English side is awarded a free kick. Beckham places the ball down on the pitch 27 meters (about 89 feet) from the goal, and a defensive wall of Greek players lines up between him and the goal. The tension is palpable. If you're a baseball fan and new to soccer, think bottom of the ninth, two outs, and the batter represents the winning run for a post-season appearance. What happened next has become the most scientifically analyzed kick in the history of soccer.

Beckham's shot left his foot traveling at about 80 mph with lots of spin on it. The ball soared over the defensive wall by a half meter (just under twenty inches). If the ball continued at this rate of speed and at the same trajectory, it would sail over the crossbar, dashing England's hopes. But just as it cleared the defensive wall, the ball moved laterally about three meters (just under ten feet) and then slowed to a speed of 42 mph as if making a mid-flight correction. To the astonishment of the Greek goalkeeper, the ball dipped into the corner of the goal. In little more than a second, England had qualified for the World Cup by riding Beckham's leg, and "Bend It Like Beckham" became a mantra.

STUDY OF THE BEND

What happened? Is Beckham some kind of magician? If so, he's not alone. In a 1997 tournament game in France, Brazilian Roberto Carlos took a free kick about 20 meters (about 66 feet) from the opposing goal. Carlos kicked the ball over the defensive wall, but so far to the right of the goal that a ball boy ducked his head in anticipation. But then the ball curved left and slipped into the top-right corner of the net to the amazement of everyone except Carlos, who frequently practiced the kick during training.

The Carlos kick inspired a 1998 article in *Physics World*, but the scientific community didn't get behind soccer until the Beckham kick, probably due to its sensational impact and the availability of high-quality video footage taken from multiple angles. Scientists at the University of Sheffield's Sports Engineering Research Group in England, Yamagata University's Sports Science Laboratory in Japan, and Fluent, a maker of computational fluid dynamics software, joined forces to learn how to bend it like Beckham. Their goal was three-fold.

"I believe that it would now be possible to design an optimum free kick for any given point outside the penalty area and to train young players to reproduce these optimum kicks," said Dr. Keith Hanna of Fluent. The scientists also hoped their research would help ball manufacturers fine-tune the aerodynamics of soccer balls so they would be more responsive to the pace and spin applied by players. Lastly, they hoped their research would lead to the design of boots that imparted spin more effectively while reducing foot injuries.

SCIENCE BEHIND THE KICK

Soccer players know that if you kick the ball slightly off-center with the front of your foot while your ankle is bent like an "L," the ball will curve in flight. The curving flight plan combined with the reduction in speed of the soccer ball was perhaps less well understood, as the study of soccer balls in flight had not been analyzed as much as, say, golf balls and baseballs. But like these other types of balls, scientists knew that soccer balls are subject to a lateral deflection effect called the Magnus force. Gustav Magnus was a German scientist who, in 1852, determined why spinning bullets and shells deflect to one side. As it happens, his explanation also works well for balls.

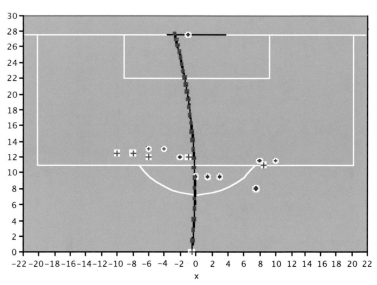

Graph shows the trajectory of Beckham's free kick versus Greece in the 2001 World Cup qualifier.

But the Magnus force didn't explain everything. Coupled with the Magnus force was a sudden transition in the airflow surrounding the ball as its speed decreased approaching the goal. During this shift between what scientists call a turbulent and a laminar flow, the amount of drag on the ball increased by 150 percent in a split second. This is what caused the ball to dip at the last moment. Just when this transition occurs varies with the rate of the spin on the ball and the

High-speed airflow
patterns around the ball.

type of surface seam pattern used on the ball. At a high spin rate, the transition occurs at faster ball speeds.

Somehow, through a combination of instinct, training, and practice, Beckham knew that this transition would occur once the ball had cleared the defensive wall of Greek players. Dr. Matt Carre of the University of Sheffield notes that "almost certainly the flow around the ball changed from turbulent to laminar several meters from the goal because otherwise our calculations suggest it would have gone over the crossbar."

Computational fluid dynamics analysis, in fact, recorded the airflow behind the ball changing with the speed of the ball, indicating that complex forces were affecting the flight path of the ball. Computer simulation also allowed scientists to deduce where the "sweet spot" of the ball was for creating maximum spin. That spot turned out to be 80 millimeters off-center, and when hit, ball spin was measured at eight revolutions per second. By contrast, kicking the ball at a spot 40 millimeters off-center reduced the rate of spin to four revolutions per second. A couple of degrees of variation in the direction of the kick or in the axis of the spin would have changed the outcome for England.

INFLUENCE OF THE BALL

Goalkeepers, meanwhile, are fooled by soccer balls that sometimes swerve in a S-shaped pattern even when the kicker puts no spin on the ball. The same group of researchers concluded after a battery of tests that the ball's panel design affected trajectory through the air. After examining balls used over a 36 year period, they discovered that drag on non-spinning balls had fallen as much as 30 percent as the balls became progressively smoother and rounder. In fact, the Adidas ball used in the 2006 World Cup has only 14 panels rather than the traditional 32. With fewer seams, says Adidas, the ball performs more uniformly. (The company used a robotic leg in its testing to obtain a consistent kick.) The larger panels provide a cleaner kicking surface with fewer "corners" that can cause balls to veer off in unwelcome directions.

What all this means is that a talented soccer player can kick the ball, spin or no spin, with more precision than ever before. Combine new ball technology with a better understanding of the physics of ball movement, and you'll soon have players bending it like Beckham almost at will. Beckham, meanwhile, continued to bend the ball practically on demand, as his electrifying 23-meter (25-yard) goal to eliminate Ecuador 1–0 in the 2006 World Cup in Germany demonstrates, proving, once again, that he is the most dangerous man in the world off a set piece like a free kick.

FOLLOW THE
BOUNCING BALL

THE WORLD CUP,
HELD EVERY FOUR
YEARS, IS SOCCER'S
GREATEST SHOWCASE.
FOR FOUR DECADES,
ADIDAS HAS SUPPLIED
SOCCER BALLS FOR
THE WORLD CUP, AND
THIS RECORD
PROVIDES INSIGHT
INTO THE BALL'S
EVOLUTION.

1970

The leather Telstar ball, with its twelve black pentagons and twenty white hexagons, featured 32 hand-stitched panels and became synonymous with soccer. The black pentagons were introduced because the 1970 World Cup in Mexico was the first to be televised and the new ball was more visible on black-and-white television. The ball made a repeat appearance in Germany in 1974.

1978

The Tango ball used in the Argentina World Cup is considered a design classic. Twenty panels with "triads" created an optical illusion of twelve identical circles. Balls used in the next five World Cup competitions were based on this design.

1982

The Tango ball in the World Cup in Spain used waterproof sealed seams for the first time. This reduced the ball's water absorption capabilities so the ball didn't get heavier during games played in wet conditions.

◄ Portuguese forward Cristiano Ronaldo (right) controls the ball in front of Iranian defender Hossein Kaabi during the 2006 World Cup group D football game, Portugal vs. Iran, on June 17 at FIFA World Cup Stadium Frankfurt in Frankfurt am Main, Germany.

1 9 8 6

The Azteca model used in Mexico was the first synthetic ball used for a World Cup. It was lauded for its better performance on hard ground, in wet conditions, and at high altitude.

1 9 9 0

An internal layer of black polyurethane foam made the Etrusco Unico ball used in Italy livelier, faster, and more water-resistant. Three Etruscan lions decorated each of the twenty Tango triads.

1 9 9 4

A high-energy-return layer of white polyethylene made the Questra model used for the USA World Cup softer to the touch (and therefore more controllable), and it was much faster off the foot for more speed.

1998

The first multi-colored Tricolore ball, used for the World Cup in France, featured a layer of gas-filled micro-balloons designed to improve the ball's energy return as well as its responsiveness and durability.

2002

With a new exterior look for the World Cup games held jointly in South Korea and Japan, the Fevernova ball also added a three-layer, knitted chassis for a more precise and predictable flight path every time.

2006

The +Teamgeist ball unveiled for the World Cup in Germany used a new thermal-bonded fourteen-panel construction that offered players an increased number of smoother surfaces for kicking in order to improve accuracy and control.

SAFE HEADERS?

by FRANK VIZARD

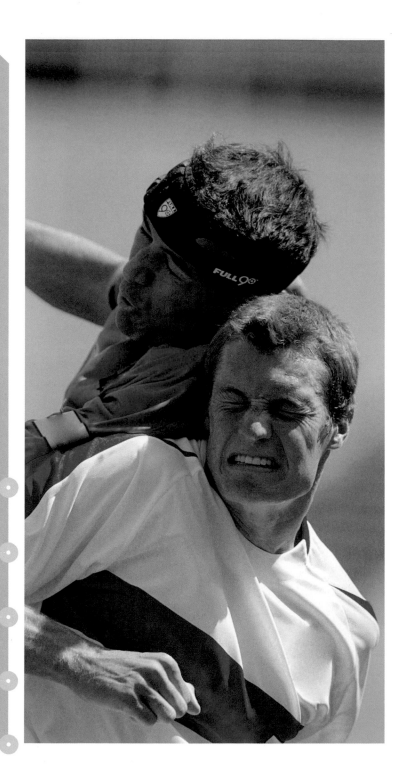

WE'VE ALL SEEN IT: A SOCCER PLAYER LEAPS INTO THE AIR AND REDIRECTS A KICKED BALL WITH HIS HEAD. IT'S ONE OF THE MOST THRILLING PLAYS IN SOCCER, AND A TEAM OF GOOD HEADERS IS SAID TO DOMINATE THE AIR. BUT IS HEAD-TO-BALL CONTACT SAFE? DOES IT LEAD TO CONCUSSIONS?

◄ Head-to-head contact, rather than head-to-ball, is more likely to result in a concussion, say scientists.

▼ Crash-test dummies are used to gauge collision impacts on all critical areas of the head.

The answer appears to be "no," according to the *British Journal of Sports Medicine* (*BJSM*), a peer-reviewed medical journal. Working with a Canadian laboratory and the International Federation of Association Football (FIFA), soccer's governing body, *BJSM* concluded that the forces associated with head-to-ball contact are not strong enough to cause a concussion. The lab, Biokinetics & Associates Ltd. of Ottawa, Ontario, examined video showing 62 cases of head impact on the soccer field and then used crash-test dummies like those commonly employed by automotive companies to re-enact the impacts. Not only are the forces involved with head-to-ball impacts unlikely to cause a concussion, said the lab, but so are elbow-to-head and hand-to-head contact.

That's not to say there is no risk of getting a concussion while playing soccer. The highest risk of concussion comes from head-to-head contact, says *BJSM*. And while such contact is often accidental, *BJSM* said that in instances where such contact seems deliberate, the sport's governing body should impose very stiff penalties.

So what can a player do to reduce the risk of concussion from head-to-head contact, accidental or otherwise? Some type of headgear is the obvious answer, but the trick is to find headgear that doesn't eliminate the header from the game. A solution endorsed by FIFA and soccer players alike is the Full90 Performance Headguard, made by a company of the same name. Full90 says its headguard, a lightweight foam layer that wraps around the head, can reduce impact forces by up to 50 percent. The headguard protects crucial impact zones like the forehead, temple, and occipital (visual-processing center of the brain) areas. The design also allows the headgear to adjust to unusual head shapes like a protruding rear cranium, for example. Fortunately, the headgear has no apparent effect on the rebound speed of the ball. "It's the only product that I have ever seen that protects the player from head injury while not inhibiting performance or providing the player with an unfair advantage," says Joy Fawcett, who played for the U.S. national women's team and is an Olympic Gold Medal winner.

THE SEAL DRIBBLE

If there is one sport where an athlete can develop a signature move, it is soccer. The great Pele, for example, had his bicycle kick. Another innovation is the seal dribble of Brazilian midfielder Kerlon Souza. The move begins when Souza flicks the ball with his foot onto his head. Then, while bouncing the ball on his head like the aforementioned seal, Souza runs through the defense, who unfailingly stop his progress by fouling him, giving his team the opportunity for a free kick, preferably somewhere near the goal.

⬥ Kerlon Souza, a forward for Cruzeiro, practicing the seal dribble during team practice in Brazil in 2007.

Swimming &
Diving

SWIM LIKE AN OLYMPIAN

UNITED STATES SWIMMING COACH BOB BOWMAN MET OLYMPIC CHAMPION MICHAEL PHELPS WHEN PHELPS WAS JUST ELEVEN YEARS OLD AND RECOGNIZED THE SWIMMER'S POTENTIAL EVEN THEN. IN THE 2004 SYDNEY OLYMPICS, BOWMAN COACHED PHELPS TO A RECORD-SETTING EIGHT MEDALS, SIX GOLD AND TWO BRONZE. IN THIS INTERVIEW BOWMAN SAYS SWIMMING IS ALL ABOUT REDUCING DRAG.

◀ Michael Phelps of the U. S. setting a world record in the Men's 200m Butterfly during the 2006 Pan Pacific Swimming Championships in Victoria, Canada.

WHAT'S THE MOST IMPORTANT ELEMENT IN SWIMMING?

In general, the key word is efficiency, meaning economy of movement. You want to get the maximum distance per stroke so you're taking the fewest number of strokes possible at the maximum rate of speed.

HOW DO YOU DO THAT?

The number one thing is to improve the mechanics of your stroke so that you're covering more water or more distance in a single stroke. That's where we start. We want to build a technical model of the stroke that has as little wasted motion as possible and in which the underwater portion of the stroke—the propulsive phase—is as effective as possible. We want to look at how you put maximum pressure on the water at the right time and how you accelerate your hand at different parts of the stroke to make the most economical use of your resources.

WHY IS THE WAY YOU HOLD YOUR HAND IMPORTANT?

One of the things you'll see in an Olympian is that they have a "feel for the water." It's one of those things that is very hard to define and very easy to recognize. If you watch their hands when they enter the water—excepting the breaststroke, of course—once the hand is submerged, there are no air bubbles around the hand. And that's what you want because once your hand is in the water, you want it to be in contact with the most solid medium possible so you get more propulsive force. If you have air bubbles under your hand, a lot of times you're "slipping" or pushing air so you're not as efficient. All of the great swimmers have that ability to get their hand in the water in such a manner they won't carry air in their hand.

IS THERE A METHOD FOR ROTATING THE HAND SO THAT ABILITY IMPROVES?

You can develop ways of entering the hand by changing the pitch or angle of the fingers and wrist so you can maximize that.

World-record holder and Olympic champion Michael Phelps swims the breaststroke leg of the men's 200-meter individual medley during the preliminary heats at the United States Open on November 30, 2006, at the Boilermaker Aquatics Center in West Lafayette, Indiana.

IS THERE ANY PARTICULAR MOTION INVOLVED?

There are a lot of factors at play. A lot was made of the Bernoulli principle (when the velocity of a moving fluid increases, the pressure exerted by the fluid decreases, and vice versa) when swimming was revolutionized in the 1960s. There is some relevance there, but what we're finding is that swimming is more about drag force than it is about wave motion. The best freestylers in the world today put their hands in the water so they're almost pulling straight back. There is a little bit of motion sideways. It's more like a canoe paddle than it is the propeller of a boat. When you watch great swimmers like Michael Phelps or Ian Thorpe, you'll see their hands go in the water with their fingertips pointed toward the bottom so that from their fingertips up to their elbow, it basically looks like a paddle. What we tell swimmers to think about when their hands go into the water is that you want to anchor your hand on a piece of water and then apply force to move your body over your hand.

THAT'S VERY DIFFERENT THAN THE WAY IT USED TO BE.

Yes. Swimmers used to be told to make a big "S" with their arms.

WHAT PROMPTED THE CHANGE?

I think people started doing better video analysis of strokes. Swimmers like Thorpe who took quantum leaps forward in their events were naturally doing this. Phelps does it naturally. That doesn't mean there isn't a 90-degree arm bend—because there is—but that occurs when the body is moving over the hand.

WHAT ELSE CAN WE SAY ABOUT ARM AND HAND MOTION?

There should be acceleration through every stroke. Most strokes start out with an extension phase where you're trying to maximize speed gained from the last stroke cycle. So as the hand goes in the water, you apply increasing pressure so that the hand accelerates through the end of every stroke, so you build momentum for the next cycle. In every stroke, there is a propulsion phase and a recovery phase, so you want to build through the propulsion stage so that you're at maximum speed at the end. This allows you to maintain velocity while you're recovering.

WHAT'S IMPORTANT IN THE RECOVERY PHASE?

It should be as relaxed as possible and as efficient as possible. In freestyle, we want the swimmer to move his hand in a straight line forward and not out to the side where you waste motion. You want everything moving forward.

WHAT ABOUT HEAD AND NECK MOVEMENT?

One of the biggest changes in swimming that's occurred in the last six years is how we changed our thinking about what the head position should be in all the strokes. Now we want the head to be carried low as a counterbalance that allows the hips to ride higher. From the 1940s through the 1970s, the thought was that if you had your head up higher, you would ride on top of the water as if you were hydroplaning. You have to be going 35 mph to hydroplane, so that's never going to happen. So we tell swimmers to be more efficient by dropping the head lower. That creates frontal resistance on the hips so the hips are held higher. At the highest level of swimming, reducing drag is our main challenge. The challenge is not how much propulsion you can create but how much drag you can reduce because drag increases exponentially as propulsion increases. The swimmers who are most efficient at reducing drag are the best. That's the key thing in Olympic swimming.

CAP OR NO CAP?

There is no question that the cap produces less resistance than your hair even if you have your head shaved.

YOU'RE REDUCING DRAG...

...by improving body position and balance.

WHAT DO YOU DO WITH YOUR BODY?

One of the things we're focusing on is how to make your body more boat-like. What can you do to make the human body travel through the water more efficiently? Our bodies are built to move on land. But in the water, the curvature of the spine tends not to be the most efficient structure. So we have swimmers flatten their backs, elongate their necks, drop their heads, and try to be in the most rigid body position possible so that it goes through the water like a torpedo. There also is a huge focus on core strength and core stability in swimmers in every stroke.

BY CORE YOU MEAN WHAT EXACTLY?

The muscles of the abdomen and lower back. We want to make sure those muscles are involved in the stroke instead of just letting the hips do their own thing while the arms pull. They are all connected. A swimmer knows when he is losing muscle tone in his torso because his hips, arms, and shoulders are disconnected, meaning they move independently. If you maintain a tight body tone throughout your body, your whole body becomes more rigid.

A high degree of body tone allows your body to move as a unit and move through the water more efficiently.

HOW IMPORTANT IS FLEXIBILITY, THEN?

Flexibility is really important because swimmers who can get into a position that makes movement through the water more fluid or easy have an advantage. Flexibility in the shoulders and the ankles is critical for getting into the most efficient position. If swimmers are tight in their shoulders, it prevents them from having a high elbow position when their hand is in front of the shoulder entering the water. If you're flexible enough to easily get into that position, you're going to have a distinct advantage over someone who has to move their body or struggle to get into that position.

HOW CRUCIAL IS THE KICK?

One area experiencing a resurgence of interest is the importance of kicking. In general, kicking is done to maintain body position. In the backstroke, of course, it is a much more propulsive force. But in long axis strokes, kicking is used much more for rhythm and maintaining body position. We place great emphasis on conditioning the legs so that they are in a state of perpetual motion during the whole swim. It's very difficult because legs have the highest level of oxygen consumption. The best swimmers are the best kickers. It gets back again to efficiency. You want to use the large muscle masses in the legs near their maximum capability and still maintain speed while avoiding lactic acid buildup.

WHAT'S THE CONNECTION BETWEEN THE STROKE AND THE KICK?

It depends on the stroke. For the butterfly, there are two distinct legs kicks per arm stroke. In the breaststroke, there is one kick per arm stroke, but that has more to do with propulsion. In freestyle, the fastest stroke is called a six-beat kick—six kicks for each stroke cycle. A stroke cycle is the stroke of both arms. Three kicks per arm.

LET'S TALK A LITTLE ABOUT AEROBIC VERSUS ANAEROBIC TRAINING.

In its purest sense, aerobic activity is exercise totally fueled by oxygen. When there is sufficient amount of oxygen in the blood, then all the energy requirements are met. In swimming, your stored energy is gone in about ten seconds and the aerobic system takes over. One of the things we do early on is to focus on aerobic training with children because while they have very little muscle

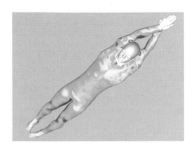

This picture highlights in yellow and orange the areas where drag affects Phelps the most.

mass and very little power capability, they are very good at endurance activities. That training carries over later in their careers because many swimming events are endurance oriented. Shorter events like the 100-meter freestyle or the 50-meter freestyle are power-oriented so less time is spent on aerobic training while more time is spent on lactic-acid-type training that is anaerobic. But even the longest-distance swimmers still need that burst of speed that comes from anaerobic training. You can't really separate one from the other, but you are trying to achieve a balance between the two that is influenced by the needs of a swimmer's particular event.

WHY DOES IT SEEM AS IF SWIMMERS ARE SWIMMING FASTER ALMOST EVERY YEAR?

In recent years, it is because of improvements in underwater kicking, particularly in the freestyle, the butterfly, and the backstroke. It's the ability to go fifteen meters underwater off each wall more quickly. Swimmers have added the underwater dolphin kick motion to their repertoires, and that's what makes them faster. There are a number of drills designed to improve the underwater kick. We like to train to kick in a vertical position, with the swimmer's head out of the water and arms crossed over their chest. We time the number of kicks they can make in ten seconds. The target number is 25. That's a pretty fast rate of kicking. Once you develop a feel for doing it like that, you can start doing it through the water and accelerate off the wall.

WHAT'S SO SPECIAL ABOUT MICHAEL PHELPS AS A SWIMMER?

The thing that makes Michael better than everyone else is that he has a highly developed technical style, and he's very conscious of that all the time. He's always very efficient, and he brings that to every stroke. There is no wasted motion. He innately does this. When he swims very fast, it looks as if he isn't trying very hard. Michael learned his technique at an early age; then he got the physical training. Combine this with a great work ethic, and you have an almost unbeatable combination.

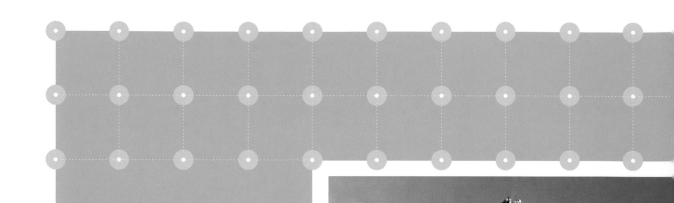

FAST SUITS

by FRANK VIZARD

SWIMMING TRUNKS JUST DON'T CUT IT IN THE POOL ANYMORE. IN THE QUEST FOR SPEED, COMPETITIVE SWIMMERS ARE TURNING TO FORM-FITTING BODYSUITS MADE FROM HIGH-TECH FABRICS. THESE SUITS HAVE DEMONSTRATED AN ABILITY TO REDUCE DRAG AND THEREBY INCREASE SPEED. IN COMPETITIVE EVENTS SUCH AS THE OLYMPICS, WHERE THE DIFFERENCE BETWEEN BEING ON THE MEDAL PODIUM OR NOT IS MEASURED IN TENTHS OF A SECOND, THE SUIT AN ATHLETE WEARS MAY BE A DECIDING FACTOR. THESE DAYS, ANYONE WHO SHOWS UP IN A PAIR OF TINY TRUNKS IS A LOSER.

◄ U.S. swimmer Jenny Thompson competes in the Women's 100m Butterfly Final at the Janet Evans Invitational in Long Beach, California on June 13, 2004.

While a number of manufacturers make fast suits, the two major companies in the field, Speedo and Tyr, have adopted different approaches to the notion of moving through the water quickly.

THE SPEEDO FASTSKIN

Speedo's Fastskin FSII, worn by U.S. swimmer Michael Phelps in the 2004 Sydney Olympics, draws on sharks for inspiration and computers for execution. Speedo's suit designers noticed that while the shark is very streamlined, the shape and texture of its skins vary across its body, and that these variations correspond to different flow conditions. Rough dermal denticles, for instance, are found at a shark's nose while smoother ones are located farther back, reflecting differences in flow at different points on the shark's body.

These observations suggested that flow characteristics also change as human swimmers move through the water. Speedo used computational fluid dynamics (CFD) computer software, originally designed for Formula One racing cars, to create a virtual flume. Virtual swimmers—computer-generated mannequins—were then added and flow patterns analyzed. Flow patterns for real athletes and mannequins in a real flume were also recorded.

Computer modeling showed that friction drag constitutes up to 29 percent of a swimmer's total drag when underwater—much more than the 10 percent previously suspected. To reduce friction drag, Speedo decided to use different fabrics arranged to mimic sharkskin, with the pattern altered depending upon the type of stroke used by the swimmer. Different suits were also developed for men and women. The Fastskin fabric works like spandex to compress the body and limit muscle oscillation. Fastskin helps reduce friction drag by creating ridges and valleys similar to those found on a shark's skin. The water skims over the ridges and skips the drag-inducing valleys in between.

At points where the body curves, another spandex-like fabric called Flexskin is used to enhance mobility. Low-profile seams join the two fabrics. Speedo suits also incorporate titanium-silicon scales on the inner forearm that grip the water better on downstrokes. Meanwhile, rubber bumps across the chest help

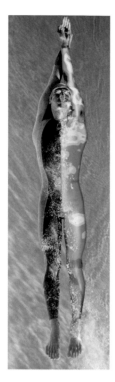

This graph shows friction points on a male body in the water.

reduce another type of resistance called pressure drag. The overall result, says Speedo, is a 4 percent reduction in passive drag for men and a 3 percent reduction for women.

THE TYR AQUA SHIFT

Swimsuit makers are as competitive as the swimmers themselves, so it should come as no surprise that Tyr thinks Speedo is all wrong in its approach. To go faster in water, you need to increase friction drag, not reduce it, says David Pendergast, one of the inventors of Tyr's Aqua Shift suit and a professor at the University of Buffalo's Center for Research and Education in Special Environments (CRESE), an institution that counts NASA and the U.S. Navy SEALs among its clients.

After studying swimmers in a special doughnut-shaped pool—a lane-wide pool that enables continuous swimming—Pendergast discovered that boosting friction drag lessens two more detrimental types of drag: pressure drag, caused by the shape of the body, and wave drag, caused by the wake created by the swimmer. Friction drag generally occurs at slower speeds, while pressure drag and wave drag occur as the swimmer moves faster.

To increase the amount of friction drag, the Aqua Shift suit uses three raised rings of equal height, called trip wires, positioned where the circumference of the body is greatest. This means one trip wire is wound around the calves, another around the buttocks, and a third around the chest. The overall effect is to keep water closer to the body to minimize water resistance. This same principle had been used by Spyder, a maker of downhill skiing suits, which developed a suit with raised piping to reduce friction drag—a suit that was banned from the 1994 Lillehammer Olympics for being too fast. Tyr says its Aqua Shift suit reduced drag by 10 percent.

THE FAST-SUIT ADVANTAGE

Do fast suits make a difference? For Bob Bowman, swimming coach for Michael Phelps and other Olympic swimmers, there is no doubt about it. "One of the main benefits of the bodysuit is muscle compression," says Bowman. "If you look at a swimmer just wearing trunks, his body doesn't look that tight, but put him in a suit and he's like a vessel going through the water. The compression of the suit gives swimmers a much better aquatic body posture."

Bodysuits also may make a difference at the finish, adds Bowman. "One of the things that occurs at the end of a race that really inhibits performance is muscle vibration. As the muscles and

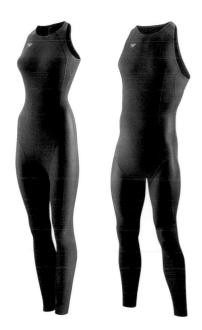

Speedo's Fastskin FSII male and female bodysuits.

Nike's version of a female bodysuit—the Nike Swim Hydra.

the nervous system fatigue, the muscles tend to vibrate and that weakens their ability to contract. The suit compresses the muscle and stops that muscle vibration, making the swimmer more efficient even when he's fatigued."

AND THE DISADVANTAGE?

Not everyone is enamored of bodysuits, however. Some early bodysuits were said to provide a performance benefit because of added buoyancy. More recently, studies suggest that bodysuits may cause body temperatures to rise and have a negative impact on performance in long-distance races in warm water. The effectiveness of bodysuits may also depend on your swimming stroke. Phelps, for example, likes a full bodysuit for freestyle swimming but wears a hip-to-knee "jammer" for the butterfly. In the butterfly, says Bowman, the jammer reduces drag better than a full bodysuit because of the way the water moves around Phelps's body. But even here, overall effectiveness may be influenced by body type, adds Bowman.

Fast suits, of course, are quickly migrating to such sports as track, where slight increases in speed pay huge dividends on the winner's podium. Whether fast suits prove to be difference between winners and losers is debatable, but competitive athletes are unlikely to scorn any technology that promises even a slight edge.

DIVING:
WHEN
GRAVITY
MATTERS

by JEFF HUBER

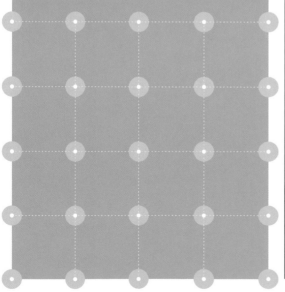

IN DIVING, 90 PERCENT
OF THE SCORE COMES
FROM THE DIVER'S
ENTRY INTO THE WATER.
BUT TO PERFORM A DIVE
WELL, 90 PERCENT OF
THE WORK COMES
DURING THE TAKEOFF
FROM THE BOARD. IN
FACT, GREAT DIVES ARE
OFTEN DETERMINED
BEFORE THE DIVER EVEN
LEAVES THE BOARD. THIS
MEANS PREPARATION IS
THE KEY.

Greg Louganis is considered by many to be the greatest diver in history, winning two Olympic Gold Medals in 1984 and 1986, an Olympic Silver Medal in 1976, and five world championships.

DIVING TECHNIQUE

Let's imagine you're on the 3-meter springboard. Obviously, with each step of your approach, your weight presses the board down and it responds by coming back up. Timing, then, is critical. Some of the better divers know how to play the board like an instrument. You have to learn how to get it to move and be one with the board. For instance, when good divers go into their hurdle, they bend their knees for as long as possible and wait for the board to come back up to its peak so that when you drop down on the end of the board, you get the maximum amount of load. As the board comes back up, your hips are forced over the top and into the rotation.

You also want to keep the core of your body—from the waist to the shoulders—very tight because if your body loosens up, it absorbs energy. So instead of getting the most out of the board going up, you wind up getting out of position and losing energy. This energy loss often happens while swinging the arms; the arm motion tends to loosen that core because the torso is often moving as well.

The direction of your flight is determined by the position of your ankles and your center of gravity on the end of the board. The two points—your ankle position and your center of gravity—determine the vector or direction your body will actually take. Position will sometimes vary according to the type of dive being performed.

Speed of rotation is determined by the amount of force used during takeoff. Speed of rotation is also affected by the tightness or compactness of the tuck, pike, or twist position. The tighter the tuck or pike position, the greater the speed of rotation around the horizontal axis. For the pike position, for example, a diver needs to get into a compact pike and get as flat as possible. Coaches don't want to see any daylight between the torso and legs once divers flatten their stomachs onto their legs.

BODY-POSITIONING PROBLEMS

Among less proficient divers, the tuck or pike position tends to open up as centrifugal force pulls it apart. When that happens, it is really difficult to finish a dive because you are out of position and you can't control it. You also want to be tight or compact along the vertical axis when you're twisting during the dive. You want to pull as tight as possible in order to get a very rapid twist. Keeping the body straight allows it to turn as a single entity. If your body core is soft, then when the shoulders twist the hips won't turn with them. That's when the legs start to come apart and very little twisting occurs. The better divers are able to pull in tight and actually increase the speed of the rotation along the vertical axis. During the twisting motion, the dive actually becomes slightly tilted along the vertical axis, which requires the diver to bring one hand up and the other hand down and then pull both arms to a T position. This motion coming out of the twist brings the body position back in line with the vertical axis and allows the diver to line up straight going into the water without any casting of the body. A cast on the entry would throw water toward the judges and cause the entry to be less "clean" going through the water and thereby cause a deduction in the score.

RELATION TO THE ENVIRONMENT

Height off the board is a key ingredient of a successful dive. Studies have shown that even if your rotation is a little slow but you have a good "top," you'll do a good dive. If you have good height, it means you were in the right position and on the right vector. Good height also means you're going to have a lot more time to come out of the dive and get your hands lined up to "rip" the dive.

The "rip" has to do with the sound the diver makes going through the water. It almost sounds like someone ripping paper. Think of the water as a piece of paper that you approach with your hands held together. As you come into contact with it, you try to tear or rip apart the paper so that you can go through it. Some divers are so good at making a clean entry that it looks as if they've displaced just two teaspoons of water upon entry, which, of course, is the purpose of the rip entry: to not make a splash. The sound, however, can be quite impressive and can influence a judge's score.

Once in the water, there is still some time for correction if necessary. Once underwater, divers routinely pull their hands down to their hips in a swimming motion that creates air pockets around the diver. If, however, the diver's feet are moving past vertical, a diver may do a "save" by bending at the waist and pushing the feet back in the opposite direction, or conversely, do a "scoop" by pulling the head back and doing a half-somersault underwater. That's been done on dives scored as perfect.

When Mark Lenzi won the Olympic Gold Medal in Barcelona in 1992, he probably wasn't the best diver at that meet, but he was the best prepared in terms of executing his takeoffs and entries. Lenzi also benefited from an uncanny ability to know where his body was at all times during a dive. Most divers count the number of taps made by the board after they've launched, to orient themselves.

Good divers are often blessed with the ability to pick up on audible or visual cues during the course of their dive. They know where they are spatially even when they are upside down. The great diver Greg Louganis told me he could hear how close he was to the water by the sound of the water sprayer used to prevent the surface of the water from becoming glassy (which affects depth perception). Other divers say they count the number of taps made by the board after they've launched off it. Olympic champion Mark Lenzi had an uncanny ability to know where his body was at all times during a dive.

Related to this cue recognition is the ability to control arousal levels. We know that when arousal levels go up, cue utilization tends to go down. A certain amount of emotional intensity can increase alertness, but at a certain point athletes get tunnel vision and they don't see their spots. So when it's time to do the big dive and win the meet, they miss their spots. I've seen kids who get so fired up that they can't control their motor movements.

Recognizing that you will miss your spots if you get too excited or anxious is half the battle. The next step is learning mental strategies such as monitoring breathing or performing physical routines that remind you to stay relaxed. At the Olympic level, the people who do the best job of that perform very well. Interestingly, 99 percent of an athlete's performance is mental, even though we spend 99 percent of our time on the physical training. That's probably because it's easier to emphasize training the body than it is to get into someone's head. We spend a lot of years perfecting performance, but there is more to it than that. As an athlete, you need to buy into the fact that there is an inner game. It's a lot of work, but the great ones buy into that and understand it. In a sense, we have to be attuned to the physics of diving but also to the metaphysics of diving!

CHAPTER 14

Tennis

POWER SERVE

by STEVE FLINK

MANY MATCHES PLAYED IN MEN'S PROFESSIONAL TENNIS ARE ESSENTIALLY EXERCISES IN BRUTALITY, FEATURING EXPLOSIVE POWER ALMOST ACROSS THE BOARD. THIS GENERATION OF COMBATANTS IS STRONG AND DURABLE, CAPABLE OF BLASTING THE OPPOSITION OFF THE COURT WITH THE EXTRAORDINARY PACE OF ITS SHOT-MAKING, AND IS ABLE TO PRODUCE BLINDING WINNERS FROM ALMOST ANYWHERE ON THE COURT.

Pete Sampras, the "King of Swing," won fourteen Grand Slam titles during his career (1988–2003).

While power prevails throughout the competitive game of tennis, it is most evident, and probably of greatest significance, on the serve. With one swing of the racket, the server can begin and end a point abruptly, keeping a rival completely off guard with the speed, spin, and placement of his delivery. The most potent servers enjoy an immense advantage over those who cannot produce the same degree of pace. The ability to generate an enormous amount of speed on the serve translates into free points, intimidates those on the receiving end who have trouble coming to terms with the high velocity, and provides a cushion in the heat of a long battle.

Big servers dominate today's game. The best players in the sport use the strength of their serve as their primary weapon. The most striking example of a champion coming into prominence in large measure because of his big serve is Pete Sampras, who was inducted into the Tennis Hall of Fame in 2007.

THE LEGENDARY SAMPRAS

Sampras demoralized more than his share of opponents with his devastating first serve, keeping them constantly guessing about where he was going with it, moving it around skillfully from corner to corner. Sampras epitomizes the modern men's champion, building his game around the explosive serve, pulling away from capable foes with the effortless ferocity of his delivery. That astonishing first serve was frequently clocked at 120–140 mph. This velocity occurs in a relatively small space when you consider that the court measures 78 feet in length and 27 feet in width for singles' tennis. The serve operates within even tighter dimensions in that the distance from the server to the opposite service line is about 60 feet.

Sampras and other stupendous servers such as Boris Becker and Goran Ivanisevic won about 80 percent of all points when they got their first serve in play. That ratio of success is a direct result of power. But where does the power come from on the serve? How do the best of the breed create such remarkable velocity with regularity?

To be sure, there are common components shared by all of the great servers, even if techniques vary among competitors. As Allen Fox, former American Davis Cup player and former tennis coach at Pepperdine University, explains, there are "three or four" sources of power that are used by players who know what they're doing.

"The object is to get the racket head moving as fast as you possibly can," says Fox. "It is done like a linear accelerator. You keep adding boosts of power from various sources until you get the ultimate racket velocity. That comes from bending your knees, throwing the racket head over your shoulder, and rotating your shoulders. That adds to the speed already coming from your legs and torso. Then you snap your wrist. Add all of those elements together, and that is where you get your power."

Australian Colin Dibley, a teaching professional in New Jersey, had the biggest serve of his era when he played the circuit in the 1970s. He describes the basis for power similarly to Fox, but adds a few of his own comments to the equation.

"You've got to use your whole body," says Dibley. "I know from my own experience that if I try to hit the serve too hard, I can lose it all. It is a matter of timing and balance. You have to transfer your weight into the ball. Players often get their weight forward too soon, and they end up hitting only with their arm."

Dibley emphasizes the importance of a good ball toss in developing a forceful serve. "To get power," he says, "you always have to go up after the ball. Wherever you toss the ball, you have to make sure you are extending up after the ball. A lot of club players toss too high and let the ball drop too low, or they don't throw the ball high enough, and therefore don't extend for power."

THE BALL TOSS

To get maximum power on the serve, the player must toss the ball out in front of his body, but not too far forward. "The ball should ideally bounce six to nine inches in front of your body if you were to let the toss drop to the ground rather than making contact with the ball," notes Dibley. "If you toss too far out in front of your body, you will be at the end of your reach and will get too much arm and very little else into the serve. But if you can meet the ball at the peak of the toss—or somewhere near the top of the toss—and place the ball slightly in front of your body, then you will get the most power."

The consistency and placement of the toss will determine the direction and pace of the serve. According to studies done by the

Vic Braden Tennis College in Cota de Caza, California, the ideal toss should be seventeen to twenty inches above the racket hand, at what is called the "peak of the reach."

Of course, the top players toss the ball the way it works for them. Steffi Graf, widely acknowledged as one of the best and biggest servers in women's tennis, had an unusually high toss, which caused her considerable trouble when the ball was blown around by the wind. Ivan Lendl had another uncommonly high toss, although he altered it over the years to make it lower.

Despite the disparity in their tosses, all servers share something more significant. No matter how high or low they make their tosses, they place the ball in the same place time after time, point after point, and therefore they get not only power but consistency as a reward for their discipline and effort. Furthermore, those who excel in the serving department share another trait that is not related to the toss—a relaxed serving arm.

THE SERVING ARM

"The arm has to be loose," confirms Fox, "because it is essentially a passive element. The arm is accelerated by the shoulders, the legs, and the torso. The arm simply allows these accelerators to work without resisting it. If the arm is stiff and you try to muscle the serve, you might actually lose power. Sampras was very loose in his arm when he served."

RACKET TECHNOLOGY

Has racket technology had anything to do with the proliferation of big serving in the modern game? The single advancement most responsible for today's blindingly fast serves, says Rod Cross, a physicist at Australia's University of Sydney, is the oversize racket head. The game was transformed as the hitting surface of rackets grew to the current legal limit of 15.5 by 11.5 inches—established in 1981. "Players hit the ball as hard as they can, and give it enough topspin to make it land in the court," Cross says. "You couldn't do that with a small wooden racket—the ball would have clipped the frame."

As Fox says, "The velocity of the serve comes from how fast the racket is moving at contact and how energy is transferred to the ball. The new rackets probably move at the same speed as older ones, but there is greater energy transfer to the ball with the newer rackets. The wide-body is stiffer. In the old days, the racket flexed backward and then the ball left before it flexed forward. Therefore, the energy was wasted in flexing the racket. These new rackets don't flex as much, so more energy is transferred to the ball."

Ram Ramnath, Ph.D., professor of aeronautics at MIT and technical

Steffi Graf, widely acknowledged as one of the best and biggest servers in women's tennis, had an unusually high toss, which caused her considerable trouble when the ball was blown around by the wind. Ivan Lendl had another uncommonly high toss, although he altered it over the years to make it lower.

advisor for the ATP tour, makes an important point when he talks about how the changing sweet spot relates to the fast-paced serving in the game today. "With the newer rackets," he points out, "the sweet spot is being raised all the time." Companies like Wilson are trying to make the sweet spot higher on the racket's strings. For very good servers, the high sweet spot, combined with the high speed of the racket, can result in great power. They make contact with the ball slightly higher on the strings for maximum power.

The most recent development in rackets relates to weight. The conventional weight of most rackets until now has been 12.4 ounces, but the trend in some of the newer wide-body frames is to make them about ten percent lighter, or ten ounces. If these lighter rackets are balanced properly, they have the capacity to contribute to a larger sweet spot—a movement that could only be a positive step for the power server.

THE SERVE RECEIVER

The advancements in rackets are benefiting players in other aspects of the game. There may well be more great power servers around than ever before, but on the other side of the net is the rapidly growing number of players who can return serves with increasing effectiveness.

Fox presents an interesting point of view on the topic. "I would have to say," he begins, "that the big servers do not enjoy as much of an advantage as they used to have. It used to be worse for the receiver. Fred Stolle would play John Newcomb in the 1960s and there would be no points to watch. The server in matches like the Stolle-Newcomb battles was dominant in a way I haven't seen since. The counterattacker gets a fair shake today because there are few grass-court tournaments and the ball is heavier than it used to be."

Clearly, the serve will remain a critical weapon across the entire spectrum of the men's game, and it has taken on increasing value among the women as well. For example, Venus Williams delivered a record-breaking serve of 129 mph in 2007.

WOMEN POWER UP

With more female players becoming taller and stronger, the power serve is now just as big a part of the women's game as it is in the men's. Venus Williams, for example, is 6-foot-1, while 1970s and 1980s star Chris Evert is 5-foot-6. In June 2005, only one of the top ten women's players was under 5-foot-8½, with the average being 5-foot-10.

Venus Williams of the U. S. serves against Vera Douchevina of Russia during day four of the Australian Open Grand Slam at Melbourne Park on January 22, 2004.

ANATOMY OF
A SERVE

by TOM COLLIGAN

NUMBER 3 RANKED ANDY RODDICK HAS THE WORLD'S FASTEST TENNIS SERVE—HIS 155-MPH SCORCHER IN 2004 SET THE RECORD—BUT HE DOESN'T LIKE TO TALK ABOUT IT. WHEN HE FIRST MET PATRICK McENROE, HIS DAVIS CUP COACH, HE SAID: "WHATEVER YOU DO, DON'T SAY ANYTHING TO ME ABOUT MY SERVE. IF I THINK ABOUT IT, I'M IN TROUBLE." HERE'S WHAT REALLY HAPPENS IN THE TWO-THIRDS OF A SECOND BETWEEN TOSS AND ACE.

◀ Roger Federer from Switzerland serves the ball to his Serbian opponent, Novak Djokovic, during the final match of the Montreal Masters tennis tournament in Montreal, Canada, in August 2007. Djokovic won 7–6 (7–2), 2–6, and 7–6 (7–2) in this upset victory against the top seed Federer.

THE WINDUP

As the toss goes up, players press their feet against the court, using ground reaction forces to build up elastic potential energy—rotations of the legs, hips, trunk, and shoulders that produce maximum angular momentum. Exploding upward toward the ball, pro players employ extraordinary timing to efficiently transfer forces from the legs, through the body segments, to the striking hand in what biomechanists call "the kinetic chain principle." Bruce Elliott, a professor at the University of Western Australia, has extrapolated the contributions of the body segments to racket-head speed (shown on next page) using 3-D videography and computer analysis. "These contributions vary from person to person," Elliott says, "but the data shows the clear importance of the trunk, shoulder internal rotation, and wrist flexion in the swing to impact."

THE TOSS

A high, confident toss made 1 to 2 feet inside the baseline allows the server to uncoil both upward and forward into the court, making contact at 1.5 times body height. For Roddick, at 6-foot-2, that is roughly 9.5 feet off the ground.

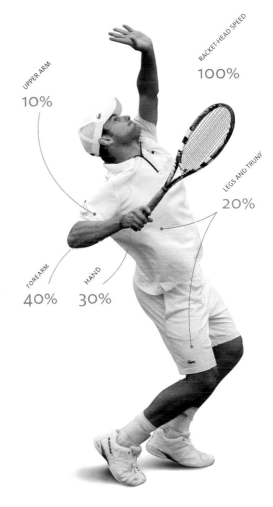

UPPER ARM
10%

RACKET-HEAD SPEED
100%

LEGS AND TRUNK
20%

FOREARM
40%

HAND
30%

A pro player looks for variations in height or location of his opponent's tosses to predict where the serve is headed—and adjusts accordingly. Top servers, however, give away nothing. "Andy can hit it hard to different corners with the same toss," McEnroe says. "Players just can't pick it up."

THE STRIKE

On a 120-mph serve, the ball is in contact with the racket strings for about five milliseconds, moving up to five inches laterally across the string plane, gathering spin. The tip of the racket moves at nearly 120 mph, though at the point of impact, a few inches closer to the ground, the racket is moving roughly 22 percent slower. The ball's additional speed comes from both the elastic energy in the rubber, which returns 53 to 58 percent of the force exerted upon it, and the racket strings (strung at an average of 60 pounds of tension), which stretch about one inch during the impact.

ACCEPTANCE WINDOW

As the ball rockets off the strings, it must travel within a very narrow range of angles to both clear the net and bounce inside the service box. Coaches call this tiny wedge of potential trajectories the "acceptance window." It shrinks as the serve goes faster—requiring incredible timing and precision to deliver a 120-mph serve inbounds. There are, however, things that the server can do (short of hitting the ball more slowly) to increase the size of the acceptance window. University of Pennsylvania physics Professor Howard Brody has identified two key tactics: strike the ball as high off the ground as possible or give the ball more topspin, which creates an area of low pressure beneath the ball (the phenomenon known as the Magnus effect) to make it nose-dive into the service court.

SPIN

A tennis ball's spin barely decreases during flight, and it actually increases when the ball hits the court. "Looking at slow-motion video, you can see that the friction of the court grabs the bottom of the ball, while the top continues to rotate, adding more spin, and converting sidespin into almost pure topspin," says videographer and tennis instructor John Yandell. The average 2,400-rpm spin rate that Yandell has observed in Roddick's 130-mph serves doubles after the ball hits the court's surface—to a whopping 4,800 rpm. This creates the "heavy ball" effect—a shot with so much movement and spin that opponents feel as though they're returning a shot put.

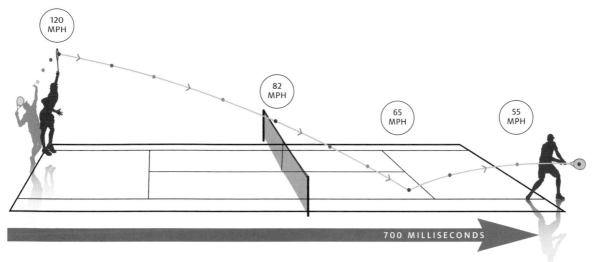

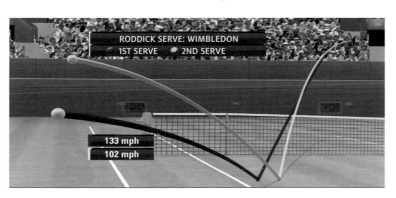

RODDICK SERVE: WIMBLEDON
1ST SERVE ● 2ND SERVE

133 mph
102 mph

VELOCITY

The serve speeds you see on courtside digital displays are measured just as the ball leaves the racket. Fortunately for returners, by the time the ball reaches them, air resistance and the friction of the court surface have diminished its speed by roughly 50 percent. Yandell has found that, on average, a 120-mph serve slows to 82 mph before the bounce, then to 65 mph after the bounce, and finally to 55 mph at the opponent's racket.

FIRST AND SECOND SERVES

Pros are successful on 50 to 60 percent of their first serves, which are faster and have flatter trajectories than their second, slower serves. At the 2007 Wimbledon tournament, Roddick nailed a 133-mph first serve (blue) that hit the court hard and bounced low with slice—sidespin that curves and draws the returner wide of the sideline.

On a second serve (yellow), Roddick employed a 102-mph "kick serve" with heavy topspin, created by brushing the strings upward against the back of the ball. This made the serve dive into the box, and it generated a high bounce that was difficult to return. First serves are flashy, but second serves are a better predictor of success: The top three players in the world are men who've won the most points on their second serve.

REVERSE FOREHAND

The reverse forehand stroke was popularized by Pete Sampras and has since been picked up by many players. This is a stroke allows a player to hit cross-court without hitting long, even though he is late to the ball. The reverse forehand starts with a strong hit with your arm extended up and behind you. But instead of hitting across the front of your body, you bring the racket back up in "reverse." The racket should end above where it started.

STRING THEORY

While the last 30 years have seen major modifications in rackets and the materials used to make them, the same revolution is occurring in the material that goes in them. Tennis rackets have traditionally been strung with gut, a natural material made from part of the intestines of cows. But now strings are made from synthetic materials such as nylon and polyester.

Synthetic strings first attracted attention in 1997 when an unseeded Brazilian player, Gustavo Kuerten, won the first of three French Opens using Luxilon synthetic strings. Soon other players made the switch— sometimes opting for a hybrid of synthetic and gut before making the switch to synthetic strings entirely. The synthetic strings let players take bigger cuts at the ball without sacrificing control. Players maintain that the synthetic strings allow them to put more topspin on the ball, so the ball stays in play despite the huge velocities generated by powerful swings. Lastly, the synthetic strings are more durable than gut.

Critics note that synthetic strings make it harder to volley and attribute the decline of serve-and-volley specialists in the game to their increased use.

PHOTOGRAPHY CREDITS

Page 14 Moodboard/Corbis. **19** iStockphoto. **20** Brian Lang/Index Stock/Corbis. **21** From top: *Kettlebells* (Sterling Publishing, Inc.); HQ Inc./www.hqinc.net. **23** iStockphoto. **24** iStockphoto. **26** Bettmann/Corbis. **32** Robert Galbraith/Reuters/Corbis. **34–36** Paul Kratter. **38** Ed Wolfstein/Icon SMI/Corbis. **41** Rich Pilling/MLB Photos via Getty Images. **42** INTOAROUTE. **43** Hans Deryk/Reuters/Corbis. **45** Gary Ciccarelli. **47** Gary Ciccarelli. **48** Bettmann/Corbis. **50–51** Bettmann/Corbis. **52** David Bergman/Corbis. **54** Cliff Gromer and Leita Rafton. **56** Danilo Ducak. **57** Paul Kratter. **58** Bettmann/Corbis. **60–62** Paul Kratter. **63–64** Bryan Canniff. **66** Dogo. **67** Chris Livingston/Icon SMI/Corbis. **68** Bettmann/Corbis. **70–71** Bettmann/Corbis. **72** Steve Matteo/AP Photo. **74** Bettmann/Corbis. **77** Peter Newcomb/AFP Photo/Getty Images. **82** Doug Pensinger/Allsport/Getty Images. **83** Melanie Powell. **87** Jeff Mitchell/Reuters/Corbis. **88** Mike Blake/Reuters/Corbis. **90** Bettmann/Corbis. **91** Andrew D. Bernstein/NBA/Getty Images. **93** Clockwise from top left: Duomo/Corbis (2); Bettmann/Corbis; Jason Reed/Reuters/Corbis. **96** Jason A. Cook/The Examiner/AP Photo. **99–101** Paul Kratter. **104** Bettmann/Corbis. **107–109** Thomas Sims/MediVisuals Inc. **112** Courtesy of Dean Golich (2). **117** Jacky Naegelen/Reuters/Corbis. **118** Courtesy of Trek Bicycle Corp. **120** Steve C. Mitchell/epa/Corbis. **122** iStockphoto. **123** Robert Steimle. **125** Rick Stewart/Getty Images. **126–127** Bettmann/Corbis. **128–129** Paul Kratter. **130** Bettmann/Corbis. **132** Robert Steimle. **133** Scott Boehm/Getty Images. **136** Row 1 – Row 2: Paul Kratter; Row 3, from left: Courtesy of Riddell; Courtesy of Protective Sports Equipment, Inc. (2) **138** Jamie Squire/Getty Images. **142** Leonard Kamsler. **144** From left: Marvin Newman/Sports Illustrated; Leo Mason/Corbis. **146** John Sommers/Reuters/Corbis. **148** Brian Brasher (2). **150** Jamie Squire/NHLI/Getty Images. **153** Jeff Gross/Getty Images. **154** Patrik Giardino/Corbis. **156** Donald Miralle/Getty Images. **159** Neal Preston/Corbis. **162** AFP Photo/Adrian Dennis/Getty Images. **164** Newscom. **166** Mel Levine/Sports Illustrated. **168** From top: Courtesy of Nike (Nike and Swoosh Design are registered trademarks of Nike, Inc. Used by permission); Courtesy of Adidas. **172** Olivier Maire/epa/Corbis. **174** From left: Goodshoot/Corbis; Nathan Bilow. **175** From top: Nathan Bilow/Allsport/Getty Images; C.J. Mueller/Swany (2). **176** Juergen Schwarz/Reuters/Corbis. **177** Flying-Chilli.com. **178** David Bergman/Corbis. **180** Dan Chung/Reuters/Corbis. **182–183** Courtesy of University of Sheffield and ANSYS Inc. **184** Yuri Cortez/AFP Photo/Getty Images. **185–187** Courtesy of Adidas. **188–189** Courtesy of Full90 Sports, Inc. www.full90.com. **190** GDA/O Globo/Brasil/Newscom (2). **192** Nick Didlick/epa/Corbis. **194** Donald Miralle/Getty Images. **197** Courtesy of Speedo. **198** Donald Miralle/Getty Images. **200** Courtesy of Speedo. **201** From top: Courtesy of Speedo (2); Courtesy of Nike (Nike and Swoosh Design are registered trademarks of Nike, Inc. Used by permission) (2). **202** Duomo/Corbis. **205** Ken Levine/Allsport/Getty Images. **208** Mike Blake/Reuters/Corbis. **211** Gary M. Prior/Allsport/Getty Images. **213** Adam Pretty/Getty Images. **214** Andre Pichette/epa/Corbis. **215** Julian Finney/Getty Images **217** INTOAROUTE (top). *Popular Mechanics* (bottom)

INDEX